COMMON
PASSAGES

COMMON
PASSAGES

Devotions
for
Seminarians
by
Seminarians

Edited by
Brian S. Gerard

Chalice Press

St. Louis, Missouri

Cover: Dan Fruend
Interior design: Elizabeth Wright

This book is printed on acid-free, recycled paper.

Visit Chalice Press on the World Wide Web at
www.chalicepress.com

10 9 8 7 6 5 4 3 2 1   98 99 00 01 02 03

Library of Congress Cataloging–in–Publication Data

Common Passages: devotions for seminarians by seminarians/[edited] by Brian S. Gerard
    p.   cm.
    ISBN 0-8272-0474-4
    1. Seminarians--Prayer-books and devotions--English. I. Gerard, Brian S.
BV4011.6.C66 1998
242'.692—dc21   98-24292
                                                            CIP

Foreword

Seminary education can come as a surprise. Students come to seminary not only for professional education but also to deepen faith and to discover community. Yet, the seminary experience is as apt to challenge faith as to deepen it. Courses in systematic theology force students to articulate beliefs that may be deeply held but still inchoate. Courses in biblical studies raise critical questions often unimagined during years of devotional reading of scripture. Courses in practical theology force students to discover whether in fact they have something helpful and true to say about God when they stand in the pulpit or sit at the bedside of a terminally ill patient.

Community is also not easy to come by in seminary. The seminary's vocation is not that of the local congregation. Faculty and administration do not see themselves primarily as pastors to the student body. Students discover that their classmates are involved in just the same stresses and doubts as they. And the human condition being what it is, considerable competition sometimes creeps into this would-be Christian community: eagerness for honors or preaching prizes or even for a date with a particular fellow student can place stress on our attempts to live out agape on campus.

Thank God, God is still God. Thank God that seminary students, like all other faithful or faith-seeking people, are invited to think on scripture, think on their lives, and pray. Sometimes the most honest prayer is that of the father in Mark 9:24: "I believe; help my unbelief."

This is a book of honest thought and honest prayer. It comes from the diverse experiences of seminary students seeking God's way for their lives (and often, almost unwittingly, also being sought).

It comes from seminary settings that are themselves very different one from another save that at each, faith seeks understanding, and the people are shaped for ministry. This book is candid and doubtful and courageous and faithful. It is a book I wish I had had when I first came to seminary as a student. I am deeply grateful that I can share it with my students now.

David L. Bartlett
Lantz Professor of Christian Communication and
Associate Dean, Yale University Divinity School

Preface

Deciding to put together this book in the middle of my Master of Divinity degree at Yale may not seem like the best idea in the world. Submerged in the usual course work and field-education of seminary, no one really has the time to add a project such as this to his or her schedule. Then it occurred to me that in the usual course work and field-education of seminary, few students can find the time to do anything else, including prayer and spiritual renewal. Moreover, if one did find the time, where would she or he look to find spiritually enriching devotional material centered on the seminary experience? It was this search that led me to call upon seminary colleagues from across the country to provide such a resource.

The goal of this project is to provide a resource for spiritual renewal for all seminary students. While no two seminary students have the exact same experience during their studies, we all have to go through "common passages" in order to achieve that sacred degree that will allow us to better serve God. It is my hope that by hearing about other students' experiences, seminarians will be able to draw strength from the fact that they are not alone.

This collection of devotions is filled with insightful and inspirational thoughts by seminarians from numerous denominations at over forty seminaries. It provides an incredible array of theological perspectives and ideas. While selecting the devotions that would be included in this volume, I was careful not to let my own theological prejudices get in the way. The theological standpoints in this book represent the variety of perspectives found at all seminaries. I invite you to be fed by all that you read, not just what you agree with. God speaks with many voices; it is important not to let our own be so loud that we cannot hear what God is saying through others.

The two years this project has taken to complete have been rewarding and challenging. I could never have completed it without the support of my wife, and favorite seminarian, Carrie Frances (YDS – M.Div. '98). I am also indebted to all the seminarians who contributed to this project. Thank you for your time and effort. In addition, I must thank the Yale Divinity School community, both students and faculty, for all the support they have given me. Special thanks go out to Deans Jann Cather Weaver and David Bartlett for their encouragement and insight, as well as to Dr. Richard Chiola and Dwight Zscheile (YDS—M. Div. '98) for their help with my initial proposal. Finally, I must thank David Polk and Chalice Press for believing in this project and giving all those who have contributed to it a chance to participate in this ministry. May this be the first of many resources dedicated to caring for seminarians.

Brian S. Gerard
Yale Divinity School (M.Div. '97)

KNOWING WHERE TO GO

I sent for all the catalogs; I called all the 800 numbers. And I waited for my mailbox to fill with letters galore: books, literary magazines, catalogs, and financial aid packages. Each package contained an application of at least four pages, and I groaned with each one. A picture for this one, an essay for all of them (of course, no two topics were the same), and having to tell why I felt called to ministry, over and over and over again.

One school offered to pay half of my way to travel across the continent. Another came to visit at a local university and offered me a glass of iced tea. One was completely rude, one bought me lunch, another was overly friendly, and that made me nervous. There was one whose students looked as if they were comatose and another whose students looked like zombies. The entire experience was completely confusing.

There was one school that offered me a free weekend with them, complete with room and board, and it wasn't all that far away. So I took a weekend off and planned a secret vacation at their expense. But little did I know what I was in for.

Oh, it wasn't what you might fear. The people were great, and I wasn't *completely* intimidated. I felt that the school would see right through me and tell me I wasn't good enough for ministry. But I knelt beside these other future seminarians (were we studying divinity or theology?), and I was at home. We prayed. Some of us cried. Jesus wept; this time with relief, and I knew that I was at home.

O God, you know me. You know the fear and you know the excitement. Thank you for the Body and Blood of Jesus Christ that bring such comfort to your flock. Amen.

Lisa A. Baumgartner
Perkins School of Theology
Dallas, Texas

1

WHERE IS GOD IN ALL OF THIS?

The blind man said to him, "My teacher, let me see again." Jesus said to him, "Go; your faith has made you well." Immediately he regained his sight and followed him on the way.   MARK 10:51–52

As I am entering my first year of seminary the farthest thing from my mind seems to be my relationship with God. I am concerning myself with my finances, where to live, supervised ministry placements, and course schedules. I am worried. I always believed that seminary would be this place where I would dwell on my relationship with God and how to teach others of God. Where did all this other stuff come from? I think about the possibility of not doing well. If I don't do well in school, does that mean I am not cut out for the ministry? Will my kinship with the Almighty be on the rocks if I make a C on a test? Sometimes these questions enter my life as I think about the years before me.

I have been taught that God is a God of grace. One who loves all even when they do not love themselves. I find great promise in this view of God. I see myself in that promise. I see someone trying his best. Someone who is not always certain of what is to come but who puts faith ahead of him and that C behind him. I am here because I have answered the call. Not to be wrapped up in the details of the world, but to be set free by a much higher standard. This idea makes me feel good. It makes me understand that God will always be here. The only reason I can't find God is my failure to lift my head above the pettiness of the world around me and look.

God, help me to have vision. Help me to see the importance of my life. Be present and help me to find visions of you in this world. Give me sight in moments of blindness.

J. Drew Johnson
Candler School of Theology
Atlanta, Georgia

NEW DIRECTION

The human mind plans the way, but the LORD directs the steps.
PROVERBS 16:9

I swore to myself that I would never enter the halls of academia again. Attending an Ivy League school had placed emotional and spiritual strains on me that had taken a long time to recover from. I had been in school for a long time and figured the bridge of higher learning had been crossed enough.

However, Jesus changed all that. He changed me. Though sometimes my plans seemed to have been in the opposite direction of God's will for my life, God eventually managed to get the point across to me. The end of my human limitations is the beginning for God to shine God's glory and majesty into my life.

It seems as if human beings spend a lifetime running from God's will for their lives. We make lofty plans for our own lives and go about filling the voids that are intentionally there. We trip, slip, and fall. It is then that we are most inclined to look up and discover that the Lord has other plans for our lives.

The first day of orientation I knew I had made the right decision. It didn't matter what others were doing around me or how my peers felt about my choice. I had the peace that one intrinsically has when one knows "beyond a shadow of a doubt" that one is in the will of God.

God, you are sovereign. You are faithful in spite of my faithlessness. From the beginning to now you have been present in my life. Continue to guide my steps that I may linger in your presence.

Charlene Hill
McCormick Theological Seminary
Chicago, Illinois

ARE YOU SURE THAT'S WHAT YOU WANT TO DO?

As they were going along the road, someone said to [Jesus], "I will follow you wherever you go." LUKE 9:57

There are at least two times in my life that I distinctly remember having my judgment called into severe question. One was when, as a teenager, I tried to ram my 1978 VW Rabbit through a three-foot snowdrift. The other time was when I told folks I was planning to give up my job as a research chemist and go to seminary. The first time they were right: the snowdrift won and I got stuck. The second time they were absolutely wrong. I would have been stuck if I had stayed in that job. It would have been foolish for me not to go to seminary.

It was hard, though, to hear Christian friends and family say things like, "What? Go to seminary and give up your well-paying, secure job? Are you really sure this is what you want to do?" The opposition was unexpected, but my face was "set toward Jerusalem," and I knew, as foolish as it seemed, that the time had come to put my career as a chemist aside.

It has been nearly three years since we loaded up the moving van and headed off to this strange and wonderful world called seminary. There have been no backward glances. God has been faithful beyond my wildest imagination. As I look forward to graduation in a few months, I face yet another unknown, but I am not alone. I serve a God who is in the habit of doing just that, calling people from the known into the unknown. Just ask Noah, Abram, Sarah, Noami, or Paul.

O God, your call has been strong in my life. I've had to trust you blindly, stumbling as I followed. As I prepare to move out again, may the penetrating light of your Spirit lead the way.

Leslie S. Horning
Eastern Mennonite Seminary
Harrisonburg, Virginia

DO IT NOW

Whoever observes the wind will not sow; and whoever regards the clouds will not reap. ECCLESIASTES 11:4

I never envisioned myself as a seminary student. As the mother of two young daughters and the wife of a husband who traveled extensively, the last thing I needed, or wanted, was any more commitments. I was a church elder, involved in a large service-based community organization, active in my eldest daughter's school as a PTA board member, room mother, and occasional classroom helper. I was also doing freelance work out of my house, and I had a preschooler still at home to boot.

When I heard God's call, I resisted. Couldn't this wait for a more convenient time, God? Maybe when the girls are a little older, or after I've had a chance to eliminate some of my existing commitments? Are you sure you have the right person, Lord?

The answer, of course, was "yes." Eventually I gave in and applied to seminary, rationalizing that now was probably no better or worse than any other time and that God would provide me with the tools, the skills, and the time (somehow!) to get everything done.

Somehow, it worked. I've learned that my idea of "the perfect time," or even the perfect person, isn't necessarily the same as God's. God provided me with everything I needed to start my new journey, and I have all the faith in the world that God will carry me through as I continue.

Lord, help me not to be so busy watching the wind or the clouds that I forget to make time for you. Give me the faith, the strength, and the courage to follow through with your plans for me, as well as the wisdom to understand them.

Nancy Lynch
McCormick Theological Seminary
Chicago, Illinois

WHY ME?

"So come, I will send you to Pharaoh to bring my people, the Israelites, out of Egypt." But Moses said to God, "Who am I that I should go to Pharaoh, and bring the Israelites out of Egypt?"
EXODUS 3:10-11

I had never really considered seminary before because I knew I was not qualified. A quick look back at my laundry list of sins was enough reminder that I would surely be struck by lightning the minute I entered the seminary door. I felt I had gifts that could be used in ministry, but my past precluded my ever seriously considering the vocation professionally. In my mind, seminary was for saints, not sinners. Even when encouraged and supported by those around me, I balked. Even as I submitted my application, I protested. Even as I was accepted, I kept thinking that the school had made a mistake. Surely God would wise up and see me for the flawed sinner that I was. Me, a minister? C'mon!

It was only as I began my first semester that I realized it was me, not God, who was holding me back. No one in seminary is perfect; we've all sinned, seminarians and otherwise. We've made mistakes; but what better way to prepare us to help others avoid the same pitfalls? God does not call those who are equipped for ministry; God equips those whom God calls. God knew the plan for me, and no amount of protesting was going to keep God from working through me. It is so easy to ask God "Why?" Instead, maybe the question should be "How?"

O God, help me to be open to trusting your call. Help me to let go and trust that you will equip me to serve your people. Most of all, remind me to continually ask you how I may best provide this service. Amen.

Kory Wilcoxson
Christian Theological Seminary
Indianapolis, Indiana

WILLING TO LET GO

But this one thing I do: forgetting what lies behind and straining foward to what lies ahead, I press on toward the goal for the prize of the heavenly call of God in Christ Jesus. Philippians 3:13–14

Forgetting about the past can be a difficult thing as we strive to answer the call of God. Eight months prior to beginning my studies, God had led me to a wonderfully dynamic ministry where I saw God do great things. Times were wonderful; I had established relationships with friends, and felt God using me in a mighty way. Yet I knew I was living on borrowed time.

As summer ended and school started, I began to ask God many questions: "Are you sure that you've called me to seminary?" and "How can you give me a blessed opportunity for ministry and then take me away from it?" My willingness to let go and let God lead me was not very strong, and although I wanted to press on for the high calling of God, I was not completely surrendered to God.

Nearly a year has passed since I asked these questions, and I have found God faithful in the midst of it all. God can and often does use the experiences of our past to shape our future if we'll let God do so.

Lord, help me to surrender my past to you. You have indeed blessed me with many good things. Help me not to dwell on them, knowing that my future is bright as I strive to follow you. Amen.

Stephen N. Rath
Asbury Theological Seminary
Wilmore, Kentucky

RUNNING THE RACE WITH GOD'S BLESSING

Do you not know that in a race the runners all compete, but only one receives the prize? Run in such a way that you may win it.
1 CORINTHIANS 9:24

The call to ministry is like running a race, but with one unique aspect that sets it apart from all other professions: There is no such thing as a finish line in ministry. Running the race in ministry is a lifetime endeavor that is a perpetual and never-ending journey. It is a journey filled with joys and unforgettable moments of success as well as sadness, frustration, and disillusionment. The recompense for this arduous task does not always come about, so we grow weary and at times discouraged.

So what is it about this race that is so appealing? It is the prize of all prizes, the assurance of knowing we have God's blessing while doing it. We are constantly strengthened and encouraged by this wonderful gift from God to help us in the work of ministry for which God has called us. It is through the peaks and valleys we experience in ministry that we realize how precious God's blessing is. We could not survive the rigors of this race without it. I know from experience.

Lord, thank you for the blessing you have bestowed upon me as I run this race. I know I could not have accomplished what I have so far without your blessing, and I am forever grateful. In the name of Jesus Christ. Amen.

Carol B. Lucas
Methodist Theological School in Ohio
Delaware, Ohio

EVER BEEN ON AN UNEVEN ROAD?

Teach me your way, O Lᴏʀᴅ and lead me on a level path because of my enemies.   Psᴀʟᴍ 27:11

Do you remember driving down a four-lane road and suddenly finding yourself in the rougher lane? The natural action to take is to switch lanes to the smoother side, right? Well, on God's highway that is not as easy as it sounds. In the midst of graduating from high school in 1980 I found myself confronted and dealing with this "call" from God on my life. I reacted in the natural fashion: I switched lanes as quickly as possible. Well, when I was thirty-four, married, with four children under the age of six, God decided to send a very distinct message to me: "NO MORE SWITCHING LANES!!!"

Here we are!!! I spent eighteen years changing lanes on God. The grace of our Lord transformed those eighteen years into experiences that have prepared me for ministry. I am blessed with experiences that I would never have had if eighteen years had not gone by. I am better prepared to minister to God's people because of my training in "Life." This journey of our lives is not easy, but as a family we are becoming more reliant on God for our daily needs. We are becoming clay so that God can mold and shape us into what God wants us to be, not what we think we should become.

We are in God's lane. There are days when I try to switch to my lane on this highway of life, but God is there to help me. God is there to help us stay focused on the smooth as well as the uneven lanes in our lives.

Lord, you shall direct our paths and our actions. Help us to know that you are actively involved in our every decision on this journey. Amen.

Mark Boyer
University of Dubuque Theological Seminary
Dubuque, Iowa

THE SEMINARY PATH

Do your best to present yourself to God, as one approved by God, who has no need to be a worker ashamed, rightly explaining the word of truth. 2 TIMOTHY 2:15

A wilderness experience we may call it. In our struggle to be faithful in truth, to meet only aridness where God is not felt. To search the balance between scholarly pursuit and faith expressed by all its mysteries. To understand God as the awakener of our senses, our deep wells of untapped love. Not to grasp onto fleeting feelings of God, but to know God, prodded by wisdom so gentle.

In our not-yet-fulfilled confidence, we are swept by grace, beyond our securities, to seek God in awesome risk. To be a worker for God, accepting unimportance as our hallmark, with creator exalted. To discover the call as a lived-out encounter in daily responsibilities, sometimes burdensome; in relationships, sometimes strained. In the discipline of meeting academic deadlines and unventured vision for ministry. In striving to live a straight path sandwiched between faith, heart, mind, theological questioning. To seek God in time that moves too swiftly, to sense the tenderness of Christ seeping into every aspect of our existence.

In our wilderness journey, God profoundly presents to us our silent brokenness, letting wholeness in Christ never be apart from our fears and doubts, from our communities and, not the least, our enemies. Our seminary path prepares us for what is to come. And it is yet where we find an oasis, that place of birth, so vital and life-giving, and the place where conviction in faith meets some of its greatest tests.

Lord, let "a straight path for the message of truth" be expressed through my life with small compromise.

Marcie McJimsey-Giarrizzo
American Baptist Seminary of the West
Berkeley, California

10

SEARCH ME

Lord, you have searched me and known me.   PSALM 139:1

Upon entering seminary, I was convinced that I knew enough to be at seminary. I had a solid academic record. I had spent enough time as a social worker toiling with homeless folks to understand the way people suffer. I had actively engaged in church and church leadership. I was all set for a smooth three-year ride toward an M. Div., which would open the door for professional ministry. I merely needed some quick Hebrew and Greek lessons, coupled with a familiarity with the volumes of Karl Barth. The education, from my perspective, was simply a formality.

Fortunately, God is much wiser than I. Needless to say, I was not as well equipped as I had supposed. Knowing this, God set me in a place at seminary where my blind spots could be gently exposed and my deficiencies brought to my awareness. Through my experience of rigorous study, encouragement from professors, dialogue with other students, prayer, and openness to God, I have come to know myself better and therefore understand myself more fully in relationship to Jesus Christ. This process of awareness, a transformation if you will, emboldens my place as a ministering person. Though this transformation has only just begun, I am now freer to be the presence of Jesus Christ to those with whom I come into contact. This would not have been possible without a God who found me, searched me, knows me, shows me, and now sends me. Likewise, it would not have been probable without the rich seminary culture medium provided by God.

Searching God, seize my heart and know it and make me know it better that I might serve you with even greater vigor.

Jeffrey W. Smith
Associated Mennonite Biblical Seminary
Elkhart, Indiana

FEED MY LAMBS

When they had finished breakfast, Jesus said to Simon Peter,
"Simon son of John, do you love me more than these?" He said to
him, "Yes, Lord; you know that I love you." Jesus said to him,
"Feed my lambs." JOHN 21:15

How could Jesus have asked such a question? Peter and the other disciples have studied under him, have seen him die on the cross, and have just finished eating breakfast with the resurrected Christ. Peter is hurt and surely shocked by the audacity of his Lord. Surely by now he knows all there is to know and has been prepared for the ministry by his many experiences. Sometimes I, like Peter, am tempted to respond, "But Jesus, I've completed my supervised ministry placement, passed systematic theology—you know that I am ready and that I love you. Why do you have to ask?"

One morning as I walked across the university campus to the seminary, I discovered in the grass a beautiful flower that I had never seen before. How often had I walked past this place, never noticing what God was doing, right in front of me? I must confess that I have approached ministry in the same way at times. In my rush and excitement to apply new teachings about systems theory and theological proofs, how many times have I betrayed my love for Jesus and my care for his people by not recognizing the ways that the Holy Spirit was already alive and active in the hearts and lives of individual church members? I am reminded and convinced that every encounter is a unique opportunity, not to display my training, but to participate with the Spirit in the nurture of another.

Lord, help me to remember what ministry is all about. Help me to be sensitive to the work of the Spirit in each person. Be near to me as I seek to feed your lambs and tend your sheep.

Matt Hamsher
Eastern Mennonite Seminary
Harrisonburg, Virginia

WHAT AM I CALLED TO DO?

With the eyes of your heart enlightened, you may know what is the hope to which God has called you. EPHESIANS 1:18

My call is very strong, yet undefined. I, like many of my friends, feel called to help others. However, my call is not as defined as that of some of my colleagues, who know that ministry is their chosen vocation. I struggle with my call, which has been dualistic in nature. I find myself called to both ministry and medicine, yet events in my life continue to direct my endeavors toward ministry.

So what is God's purpose and direction for my life? I don't know! This not knowing elicits a wide spectrum of emotions, ranging from fear to exhilaration, about what my future holds in store. Wherever the path leads, I am confident that I will be fulfilling God's will to serve others. I also know that my faith has grown by leaps and bounds as I have explored who I am and what I have to offer the world around me.

God, give me the patience to discern your will. Grant me the wisdom to use my strengths and gifts toward your service—knowing that whatever vocational avenue I follow, your unconditional love will support me.

Jason Gottman
Vanderbilt Divinity School
Nashville, Tennessee

WHAT ARE YOU DOING HERE?

...and after the fire, a still small voice. So it was, when Elijah heard it, that he wrapped his face in his mantle and went out and stood in the entrance of the cave. And suddenly a voice came to him and said, "What are you doing here, Elijah?"
1 Kings 19:12b-13, NKJV

W hat are you doing here?" asked God of Elijah (or is it my mother exclaiming, "What do you mean you're going to seminary? God isn't a woman!"). Throughout this first semester at seminary the voice echoes within my head. Fifteen years ago a friend told me, "What you really want, you know, is to go to seminary." My response was, "You've got to be kidding. I don't even believe in God." Today I am engrossed in Old Testament exegesis, the Gospel of Thomas, Augustine and the problem of evil, and Asian feminist liberation theology—and I almost forgot how I got from there to here. I lose sight of a call so clear and strong that at age fifty I left my teaching career and home in Connecticut to answer it.

"What are you doing here?" I ask myself. Who am I to be entering seminary: I who grew up in a religious vacuum? I who have been a profound agnostic for most of my life? How can I be called to ministry? Am I listening to God's query, or the voice of my mother reverberating in my mind? Even as I ask the question, I know that to discern the answer, I must slow down. Augustine, Thomas, and Chun Hyun-kung must wait so that I can take the time to be present to God. Only then will I be able to listen to that still, small voice through which God has led me to this place.

God, allow me to separate the internal voice of fear and doubt from your call. Help me put aside my studies and take the time to discern your presence in that "still, small voice" through which you guide me.

Linda Carleton
Bangor Theological Seminary
Bangor, Maine

WHY ME LORD?

O Lord, you have searched me and known me. You know when I sit down and when I rise up; you discern my thoughts from far away. You search out my path and my lying down, and are acquainted with all my ways. PSALM 139:1-3

I am just past the halfway point of my seminary journey, and as I reflect back upon the road that brought me this far, I never cease to be amazed at just how twisted and curvy, and sometimes dangerous, that particular road has been. For me, the question hasn't been so much "Why has God called me to this place?" Rather, it has been "Why did it take me so long to figure out that this is where God wanted me?" There are no good answers, and there is no logic as to why an ex-grave digger/ex-rock musician/ex-accountant such as I would find himself at seminary. And as I share these feelings with my fellow seminarians at Eden, they too wonder where the logic is in all of this. But God knows why, and God does understand our questioning. And sometimes our God is beautifully illogical! This is where our faith steps in and takes that final mile into the ministry, into that uncertain land of challenge and mystery, of satisfying fatigue and a "peace that passes all understanding."

Gracious and loving God, all of the talents we possess are truly gifts from you, gifts of your love and grace. As we enter into your service, help us to use these gifts to the glory of your kingdom, and to the honor of your Son, Jesus Christ. Amen.

Steven Staicoff
Eden Theological Seminary
St. Louis, Missouri

ALL READY, BUT NOT YET

But if we hope for what we do not see, we wait for it with patience.
ROMANS 8:25

After nearly a year out of seminary, I still do not have a church job. My life-partner is Canadian; and as I was nearing the end of seminary, we realized that our lives, for at least the next few years, would find us in Canada and not the United States. At first, both of us were loath to make the move, knowing that my goal of parish ministry in the United Church of Christ could not be fulfilled outside of the States. But as I neared graduation and was preparing for my denominational ordination interview, a change came over me that altered my perspective.

What happened was this: I realized that I could and would be a minister for Christ wherever I went, even if that meant I had to put off my immediate plan to work in my beloved church. In prayer, I came to understand that by following Stèphane to Canada I was following God's plan for me. I realized that it indeed had been my plan to go right into UCC ministry, but that God, through the love of my partner, was clearly calling me forth into a new land.

Though I have to admit twinges of envy as I celebrate with seminary friends their ordinations and installations, for the most part I am content. I trust that God's Spirit is guiding me to the places where, and people with whom, I am the most needed (and most need to be).

Triune One, grant me the patience to see your plan for me when my own plans seem to fail. Fill me with hope that you will use me wherever I am. I give my life to you.

Read Scudder Sherman
Harvard Divinity School
Cambridge, Massachusetts

WRITING MY LIFE

Those who are spiritual discern all things, and they are themselves subject to no one else's scrutiny.   1 CORINTHIANS 2:15

Journals stand like deserted houses in the ordered neighborhood of my bookshelf. Although I had begun numerous journals, the discipline of journaling continued to escape me until I was handcuffed to the experience by several seminary professors. Reflecting on ethical essays, exploring the ebb and flow of my spiritual life, experimenting with sermon ideas—journaling became a crucial cog in the wheel of my spiritual disciplines.

Now I won't give it up. Some pages contain prayers. Others, brave poems. Some bask in a compliment, whearas others gripe and groan. Some entries explore a sermon idea or deliberate the puzzlement of a scripture passage. Writing my thoughts, reflecting on my experiences, pondering new ideas, venting my frustrations—looking at the real me in the mirror of my journal has helped me know myself better.

"Experience is the best teacher," they say, but I have come to value the *reflection* of the experience as much as the event itself. The disciplined, honest, private ponderings of what I am learning and who I am becoming is an investment of my time with rich returns. Seminary is not just about learning. Seminary is about discerning.

Holy God, you are the God of all wisdom, and you promise wisdom to those who ask. Write upon the pages of my heart today and reveal more of yourself and more of myself to me. Amen.

Charlotte Vaughan Coyle
Brite Divinity School
Fort Worth, Texas

CLEARING THE LAND

Let anyone among you who is without sin be the first to throw a stone at her. JOHN 8:7

I am surrounded by stones. I think of the foundation of our newly acquired rental house. I look at the upturned subsoil of the seminary community, a fact of life on our campus where work is always being done: cables laid, jackhammers going off and on, bulldozers clearing land. I see stones of all shapes and sizes, names I once knew that now fail me, protrude from the soil. I think back to simple joys, flat rocks I could skip across a lake, how they would catch air and go forever, walking on water. And I have regret too: I see myself ten years old, arguing with a neighborhood bully, ending with a long throw, the stone striking him in the base of the head, blood flowing freely from the wound.

The words of Jesus hit hard. Forceful, they come from the Rock himself. They remind me that sin is always there, crouching, waiting, embedded in our lives like rocks in the soil, wedded to the earth's being. And now I have a choice in the matter. I can submit to the beauty of God's creation, or grab it and craft evil.

The rock is in my hand. I feel its heft. I cradle it. What do I do now?

Purge us of sin, O Lord. Grant us wisdom in the daily struggle with school, friends, and family. May the Chief Cornerstone strengthen us, this day, now and forever. Amen.

Duke S. Stewart
Virginia Theological Seminary
Alexandria, Virginia

GOD IS IN THE FACES

O send out your light and your truth; let them lead me; let them bring me to your holy hill and to your dwelling.   PSALM 43:3

I am finally here, and I can hardly believe it! After twelve years of talking, dreaming, and praying about going to seminary, I really am finally here! The campus is beautiful. My classmates are wonderful, incredibly bright and kind, articulate and funny, and I love them all. I am working harder that I ever have. And I am having a grand time! I love the classes and the discussions before, during, and after them. I am eating, breathing, sleeping, and dreaming the word of God, and I can feel it working in and on me.

I find myself in the presence of God daily and moment by moment. I hear God whispering in my ear as I walk through the grove in the late afternoon sunlight. I see God in the face of the senior who is helping me with my first exegesis paper, and a fellow junior with whom I share my class notes. I sing in the choir for the first time since I was a teenager, and the music we make is sometimes so sublime that it breaks my heart, and it doesn't seem possible that we could have made it!

I understand now how strongly most priests feel about their seminaries and about the people who shared this incredible experience with them. This place has a way of stripping life to its barest essentials and showing us who we are and what we care most deeply about. Seminaries are holy ground because so many people over the generations have found in them communities of the heart, where the grace and courage to look for and upon the face of God and to see God in the faces of fellow seminarians and professors, and ultimately of everyone, is powerfully present.

Marty Conner
Virginia Theological Seminary
Alexandria, Virginia

COMMUNIONITY

Those who eat my flesh and drink my blood abide in me, and I in them. JOHN 6:56

As someone who considers himself a theologically traditional Protestant (whatever *that* means), I used to approach communion much the same way that many, if not most, Protestants do: as a commemoration, or memorial, of Jesus' death and sacrifice. Thus, the passage from John was always a bit of a mystery to me. It was safe for me and manageable as long as I saw it as pure allegory. The practical application of it was particularly comfortable: consuming my *own* wafer and juice out of my *own,* personal, sterile little plastic disposable cup.

Until I attended a Catholic Mass. As all came *forward* to the wafers and the *one* cup which *everyone* (Yikes! Germs!) was drinking from, as I heard the soft shuffling of feet moving toward the cross over the singing and the soft priestly chant: "This is the body of Christ broken for you; this is the blood shed for you," a profound change came over me. I had the sudden realization that, only as *everyone* was partaking together, *as community,* the wafer and wine somehow mysteriously was transformed into the flesh and blood. It was the *body* doing it *together* that made it so, and not any particular prayer. Everyone sharing together in this moving ritual made it much more than a mere commemoration; the mystery became accessible while remaining profound. I don't pretend to possess any truth behind the mystery of communion; far from it. But that night I touched upon something deeply outside of myself: I realized the secret behind *communionity.*

Lord, I give you as much thanks as I am capable of giving for the body and the blood. May I know fully and honor completely your desire for community.

Matthew R. Henry
American Baptist Seminary of the West
Berkeley, California

BECOMING COMMUNITY

On the contrary, the members of the body that seem to be weaker are indispensable.   1 CORINTHIANS 12:22

It was several weeks into my first semester at seminary, and I felt lost. After moving across the country, leaving my church home and friends, not to mention a well-paying job, it felt as though I had become anonymous, just one more student, with talents and skills that no one knew about. Then one day after class, I tripped on a step and fell down on an ankle that swelled rapidly. Students rushed to my aid, and I ended up with a chauffeur-driven ride to the emergency room by a student I hardly knew.

Hobbling out of the emergency room, I gained a new perspective on what it means to be in Christian community. Community can come when we least expect it, often when we show our weakness. Ardyss, the student who drove me to the hospital, became a close friend; together we began a weekly potluck supper for students to gather informally for fellowship. Soon, I gained enough courage to ask others to join me in a small covenant group to explore the issues we faced as seminarians and to support one another in our journeys of faith following our calls. Later, we newcomers began to be known to the rest of the community, and our gifts were used.

As I enter my final year of seminary, I see that God's hand was leading me into the community from weakness rather than from strength.

God our sustainer, help us to be members of the body in both weakness and strength. Let us be the visible signs of your whole church universal through the love we show one another.

Renee Marie Rico
San Francisco Theological Seminary
San Anselmo, California

THE COMMUNITY OF GOD

...that they may be one, as we are one. JOHN 17:22

Chapel services are very interesting. At St. Paul School of Theology, students have the opportunity to preach during their last year. What they have to say is always fascinating: their way of preaching, their interests, their stories, their theology. I am especially aware of the occasions when students' sermons center around controversial issues, each taking the opposite side of an issue. Diversity of opinions—that is seminary.

On one such occasion, I had the blessing of assisting at communion. As people came to take the elements, I saw many faces. People that I knew disagreed with the preacher took communion alongside those who agreed. This diversity was also present in those assisting with the elements. One thing did not change from person to person: a smile of gratitude because of the sacrifice of Jesus Christ.

Even when we disagree on many things, Christ unites us. It is that Spirit of love that I have felt since arriving at seminary. I took a leap of faith in coming here. Yet, I found a new family, new friends, a new life. This is what I have found in this place. Community—that is seminary.

I think about Jesus' prayer now and find it refreshing. He prayed to God that we become one. One even in our differences. One in love.

Jesus, teach us to pray like you. Teach us to act like you. Teach us to be one.

H. Eduardo Bousson
Saint Paul School of Theology
Kansas City, Missouri

ANSWERING THE CALL

For many are called, but few are chosen.   MATTHEW 22:14

M oving into seminary life is at first exciting, especially if you are fortunate enough to live in campus housing, which turns into instant community as relationships quickly develop. But by the end of the first year, living and studying with the same people starts to get old. Patience can wear thin, nerves fray; you get sick of the constant interaction with the same people. Early on, Charlie, a fellow seminarian, had said, "These are the best years of our lives." At times I wasn't so sure.

Until the night Gail passed away. At fifty years of age, one of our sisters died of a stroke. That easy, that quick. I got the call at midnight from someone in the next building as Gail was being carried away, still alive, to the hospital. The call went out like the cry of Paul Revere. I immediately called someone else, who called someone else, who called...

At 12:30 a.m. we dragged ourselves into the seminary chapel, about twenty of us, exhausted from lack of sleep due to papers and tests. We immediately started praying, singing hymns, and praising God. We did what a seminary community should do, what we were being trained to do. Funny how there are really no set hours to do this sort of thing. Gail died, but we never felt the same again. We realized deeply our being chosen. Charlie was right: these are the best years of our lives.

Lord God, teach me to have the patience, love, and understanding with others that you have with me. Help me to fully grasp the sense of being chosen.

Matthew R. Henry
American Baptist Seminary of the West
Berkeley, California

LOVE THAT WILL NOT LET ME GO

The Lord is their refuge.   Psalm 14:6

I left the seminary sobbing. The semester was over and I was exhausted. I knew the "kids" were having a semester's-end lunch, and I felt the pain of being the oldest in the school, including all of the professors! I loved my young friends, and I could have stayed for lunch, but there were two hours of travel ahead of me, a promise to go to an early "grandson" baseball game and then to choir practice at the church. Why hadn't I gone to seminary years ago?

My precious husband had supported and encouraged me to finally answer God's call because he wanted me happy. Was I doing the right thing? Would I later be sorry that I did not spend this extra time with him?

All at once I felt a strong urge to turn off the road and follow a sign to an old, heavily piled antique shop. I entered the shop with a weary heart, but soon I was visiting nonstop with a lady my age who shared her "story" with me. Her faith was strong and her eyes sparkled. Then I found myself sharing my feelings and my pain. I left the shop with a new friend and her assurance that God would continue preparing me for the work ahead. As an exciting bonus, I found the exact pair of ceramic cocker spaniels that I had been seeking for a gift.

Thank you, God, for your love that will not let me go, and for your miraculous nudges toward places of healing.

Merilee Berry
Phillips Theological Seminary
Enid, Oklahoma

TO MY PARTNERS IN MINISTRY

I hope in the Lord Jesus to send Timothy to you soon, so that I may be cheered by news of you. I have no one like him who will be genuinely concerned for your welfare. All of them are seeking their own interests, not those of Jesus Christ. But Timothy's worth you know, how like a son with a father he has served with me in the work of the gospel. PHILIPPIANS 2:19–22

To my dear friends in Christ, God's Holy people, partners in the proclamation of the gospel,

I thank my God whenever I think of you for your partnership in the gospel and for ministering to my need. When I began my theological studies, I had the misconception that I was doing this on my own. How wrong I was, for it has only been by the grace of God, made effective in your ministries, that I have been able to endure the challenges of seminary. I know now that I cannot serve without also being served. As part of the church, the one body of Christ, we build up one another to proclaim the gospel. You have prayed for me, fed me, led me to worship, provided me with recreation, paid bills for me, and nurtured me in my weariness. I thank God for these gifts of service you have given. In all this, I have been urged on in my partnership in Christ's ministry. Now, when it is 3:00 a.m. and I have a paper to finish, a test to study for, and a cold coming on, I am not shy or embarrassed about accepting your service to me. Rather, I accept it as I think you intended, as an offering to God, so that I might not be taken out of service, but rather be a partner in service with you.

Gracious God, bless those who, in service to you, are ever helping seminarians to be faithful to their calling in your shared ministry.

Ashley Abraham Hood
Perkins School of Theology
Dallas, Texas

25

LONELINESS

Remember, I am with you always, to the end of the age.
MATTHEW 28:20b

I think the feeling that hurts us most is loneliness. The loneliness that we feel when we sin. We feel as if the whole world falls apart, that we are not worthy of our calling, that in sinning we reject God. Loneliness because some of us are far from home, and that separation makes us feel vulnerable, and sometimes we simply find it hard to trust in someone new. Loneliness when we pray because we cry to God and there is no answer nor conversation. Loneliness when we pray because we as ministers see so much pain and sorrow and injustice, but nothing seems to change. Yes, sometimes we feel lonely.

When I feel lonely like this I grab my necklace (which is a cross) and pray. It helps me remember Jesus and how lonely he felt at the cross. It helps me remember the painful prayer at Gethsemane and his final cry, "O God, my God, why have you forsaken me?" It helps me to feel less lonely because Jesus felt like I do, and because of that, he is with me.

Ministry is a long and hard journey. Expectations surpass reality. Therefore, whenever we feel lonely, let us remember the cross. Jesus is with us.

God, you are with us, but sometimes we do not feel you by our side. Would you help us remember you? Would you help us remember the cross?

H. Eduardo Bousson
Saint Paul School of Theology
Kansas City, Missouri

ROCK BOTTOM

It happened in the second semester of my first year. I was feeling down and alone and didn't share that honestly, even with my friends and therapist. After our community lunch, I went home and feeling in another state of mind, farther from God than I have ever felt, tried to kill myself. I didn't feel competent for ministry, for seminary, for life. I knew immediately that I had made a mistake and that I really needed help. It was a rather lame attempt in the first place, and I called the school psychiatrist, who ordered me to the hospital.

Now I really felt like a failure. My mentor in ministry was so angry with me that she refused to talk to me. I needed a leave from school to get some help. I was so overcome with embarrassment that I didn't want anyone to know what had happened, especially my seminary friends, faculty, and administration, but most especially, God.

It's no surprise that I couldn't keep it from God. God was there all along. And my friends followed. I was able to miss some time from school without losing everything. A few days after I was put on medication, I was back to myself and realized that I had an illness called depression that was no different from my high blood pressure. I still kept it quiet, until now.

I thought some of my seminary brothers and sisters would understand. My seminary community gathered around me with tremendous love. As Jesus said, "Do not let your hearts be troubled. Trust in God; trust also in me." (John 14:1, NIV)

O God, it's hard to be a human. But this is what you called me to be. It's hard to hurt and feel alone when I think I'm supposed to be above all the rest in my "holiness." Help each one of us to remember that we are never alone, even in the worst of times.

Lisa A. Baumgartner
Perkins School of Theology
Dallas, Texas

SMASH!

Yet, O LORD…we are the clay, and you are our potter; we are all the work of your hand. ISAIAH 64:8

This is how I figured seminary works—junior year God forms you, and middle year God fires you, so that by senior year all that's left is to slap on the glaze and put this jar out on the shelf. When fall term opened, I don't think there was a happier student on campus than this senior. The final hurdle was supposed to be cleared by Thanksgiving, when my Commission on Ministry would inform me of their decision regarding my application for ordination, but in my mind it had become a done deal.

Three weeks into the term, the phone rang. I was napping between all-nighters, but my roommate woke me and put the receiver in my hand. A voice on the other end informed me that the Commission had decided not to go ahead with my application. "This is a nightmare, right?" "No. I am afraid not." I cried. I pleaded. "Sorry, but our decision is not negotiable."

Smash! It was almost audible; the beautiful jar fell from the shelf and shattered into a million pieces. I dragged myself to class, but there were potted plants that were more present than I was. A friend came up and asked, "Did you ever wonder why Jesus broke the bread before He blessed it?" Those words got through to me. The next few months were almost impossibly painful, but full of Jesus' presence! I put my call back in his hands, and he has blessed it. I am going to be a priest, and a far better one than I would have been before. All glory to God.

Thank you Lord, for making your strength perfect in our weakness. Keep me in the shelter of your loving hands that I may ever give you glory. Apart from you, I can do nothing!

Lori F. Sbordone-Rizzo
Trinity Episcopal School for Ministry
Ambridge, Pennsylvania

TAKE THOU AUTHORITY

Do not fear, for I have redeemed you; I have called you by name,
you are mine. ISAIAH 43:1

The ordination process is a roller coaster of emotions. Daydreams filled with visions of the ordination ceremony. What hymns will be sung? When will the tears begin to flow down my face? As each year passes the anticipation grows. What a glorious day it will be! Soon daydreams are intertwined with ordination interviews and doctrinal examinations. "So what is your understanding of the nature of God? Please keep your remarks to two pages or less." Watching the tremendous influence of the pastor leaves me shaky. Who am I to represent the church? O Lord, am I up for the task? Will I bring your loving Spirit to someone's deathbed? Can I bring comfort to a child who has just lost his mother? Someone said my sermon inspired her to make a change in her life. O Lord, how do I dare bring counsel or comfort in your name? How do I dare to preach in your name? I dare because I know that you are with me. You, Creator of all, will use my words and actions as you choose. I trust you to use me for your purposes.

Take thou authority,
How do I dare?
The burden of responsibility,
The commitment to care.
Take thou authority,
How do I dare?
Because I know, dear Lord,
That you will be there.

Lord, thank you for calling me to serve your people of faith. Help me sense your Holy Spirit as I live out that call. Amen.

Nancy Cushman
Claremont School of Theology
Claremont, California

CONVERSIONS AND DETOURS

A new heart I will give you, and a new spirit I will put within you; and I will remove from your body the heart of stone and give you a heart of flesh. Ezekiel 36:26

When I entered seminary, my life was under control. I knew exactly how it was going to play out: courses, internship, ordination, church job. I didn't know much about God, but I felt confident that I could perform the tasks of ministry. By my last year of seminary I had passed all my denomination's requirements and was ready to be ordained; I just needed to make one phone call to set the process in motion. Inexplicably, I couldn't do it.

You see, I had encountered God at seminary: first in the graceful words of the Old Testament, and later in Jesus' call to discipleship. Over time, I recognized that God had come first—whereas I had been starting with myself. Plus, my denomination affirmed the dignity of every person but found it hard to speak of God. The fall before graduation, I realized with pain that I needed to change denominations.

It has not been an easy process. I have been embarrassed by this unexpected detour in my spiritual journey. I have lived on the financial margin. I have not always been comfortable in my new denomination. And yet, I would do it again, regardless of the consequences. I still hope to be ordained, but I now know that I'm not in full control of my life. God has put a new heart in me, and ironically, I have done more than I ever thought possible.

God, thank you for all the changes you put me through. Help me open my heart to you and respond willingly, no matter where your call takes me. Amen.

Karen Cassedy
Wesley Theological Seminary
Washington, D.C.

OPPRESSION

Again I saw all the oppressions that are practiced under the sun.
Look, the tears of the oppressed—with no one to comfort
them! ECCLESIASTES 4:1

After going to a movie, a seminary classmate and I go out for dessert. Our waiter directs all inquiries to my classmate, even when I am the one asking the questions. All of this might be overlooked, except that I am black and my classmate is white. I can't believe this is happening and dismiss an all-too-familiar scene.

It is a couple of months later, when we are discussing the noticeable distance in our relationship, that I haphazardly journey back to that night. Surprisingly, my classmate also was observant of the waiter's response. In defense of her own actions, she states that she tried to redirect the waiter to me.

However, it doesn't sit well with me. As our seminary attempts to teach us to be active in the struggle for justice, I'm discontented with my classmate's actions. And I am disturbingly bothered by my own passiveness. If we cannot effectively implement and practice what's learned in seminary, then why are we here? If we cannot integrate Christian ethics into practical living, why are we here?

Frederick Douglass, a black abolitionist and active participant in the struggle for justice for all said, "If there is no struggle there is no progress. Find out just what any people will quietly submit to and you have found out the exact measure of injustice and wrong which will be imposed upon them." That struggle has room for all.

Lord, employ your servants to tear down walls of racism, classism, and sexism. Where there is injustice, may we sow seeds of justice. May we be witnesses of your reign throughout the world.

Charlene Hill
McCormick Theological Seminary
Chicago, Illinois

FAILURE

Deliver me from that which may hurt or destroy me, and guide me along the paths of love and truth. PSALM 139:24, paraphrase

With us in our deepest failing,
God of love, to you we cry:
help us know your love prevailing;
heal our wounds, us sanctify.
When we call to you in anguish
send your spirit to our side,
that our pain may not us languish
but to growth become our guide.

You alone know all our story,
things both done and left undone,
yet you come in flash of glory,
granting gifts to everyone.
Save us from the time of trial
and transform us in your ways,
and we'll turn from pain's denial
to your worship, love, and praise.

Take our worry, grief, and sadness,
make them lessons valuable,
that we may know more than gladness,
in your joy ineffable.
Strengthen us in faith and wisdom
that we may forever tell
in Christ Jesus your reign is come
and, in truth, all shall be well.

Suggested Tune: *Abbot's Leigh,* Cyril Vincent Taylor

Tender, loving God, you know all my lights and my shadows. Enliven and strengthen me by your many blessings. Amen.

J. Barrington Bates
The Church Divinity School of the Pacific
Berkeley, California

32

HOW DISCOURAGED ARE YOU?

[He] died for us, so that whether we are awake or asleep we may live with him. Therefore encourage one another and build up each other as indeed you are doing. 1 THESSALONIANS 5:10–11

How discouraged are you?" His question caught me off guard. He really wanted to know. He had asked how I was doing as we headed in for class. I casually mumbled something about feeling discouraged. He stopped, squared up to me and asked, "How discouraged are you?" His eye contact said he was more than curious—he was concerned. His tone was firm, gentle, undemanding. From how he stood and how he spoke I knew that he was really asking, "Are you feeling so discouraged you want to quit?" He read through my subtleties and met me where I was: on the edge of a decision to drop out of seminary. He asked...and then he listened.

He listened to my frustrations with endless reading assignments and complaints about balancing youth ministry with my training to be a minister. He listened. He just listened. That's all I remember. It was hardly a ten-minute conversation. But I was a new creation. He was Christ to me that day—journeying out from the ninety-nine to be with me in my discouragement. Through him God brought me back to God's self—back into a stability centered on the knowledge and experience of God's love for me.

Good Shepherd, you are so very loving and patient. Thank you for never leaving me too long on my own before bringing me back into the knowledge and joy of your presence. Please open my eyes to perceive your help and make me ever ready to be your help to those you've placed in my life.

Jennifer Swick
Luther Seminary
St. Paul, Minnesota

WHERE IS THE JOY?

I have said these things to you so that my joy may be in you, and that your joy may be complete. JOHN 15:11

A friend of mine is in her second year of seminary and is confronting some challenges that make it difficult for her to focus on her studies. She asked me wearily, "Where is the joy?"

Having undergone quite a few problems while on my own seminary journey, I have found God has taught me a few things about recovering joy.

Jesus promises joy to his disciples in the midst of troubles. In John 15:7-11, Jesus gives us the "how to's" of joy: *Abide in me, and let my words abide in you, ask for what you wish.* Spending time with God in prayer, asking God for peace, and being thankful for God's presence can restore joy to a troubled heart.

A positive attitude and gratitude lead to joy. Resolve not to allow the hard times to erase your fellowship with Christ, but rather, live with Christ. Joy will not only return but grow deeper and stronger.

Lord, help me to trust in your loving presence during trying times. Amen.

Eleanor A. Morgan
American Baptist Seminary of the West
Berkeley, California

CLOSER TO GOD

But God gives all the more grace; therefore it says, "God opposes the proud, but gives grace to the humble." JAMES 4:6

I am a second-year student at Saint Paul School of Theology, studying for a Master of Divinity degree. My third semester in graduate school seemed to begin very nicely. I had a fairly acceptable schedule of classes and assignments, until I looked at the month of October. I could not believe the amount of work that I had to do that month! Have you ever had a month that seemed as if it would never end? Have you ever wanted to just quit the ministry and deny your call? I sure questioned my call during that month. Between academics, ministry, and personal life, I felt that I had little or no life. And where was God during my struggles?

I found God's help during a time of great stress studying for my last assignment that month. I have studied countless hours throughout my life, but never did I think of God as being with me, helping me study. While studying that day and night, I sang along with Christian music, took time to pray on my knees, and thanked God for all of the good things I had received in my life. I cannot express the feeling of joy that I felt as I studied while glorifying God. Many times in my life I have accepted the glory for a good grade and have not thanked God properly. Although we all struggle with balancing our busy schedules, I believe that taking time out to pray, sing, and thank God while studying is one of the best ways to learn about God. Try it. It works.

Dear God, thank you for everything you have given me. Guide me to the path you would have me follow. Remind me to be humble in all my endeavors. Amen.

Jeremy T. Vickers
Saint Paul School of Theology
Kansas City, Missouri

LAMENTING EQUALS HEALING?

Ask, and it will be given you.   MATTHEW 7:7

A very useful method for dealing with the stress of seminary life (and life in general) is to pray in the form of a lament psalm. This allows one to "vent" one's frustrations in a Christian context and at the same time raise them up to God. The "quality" of artistic expression in one's personal lament to God is not as important as the act of expression itself. However, it does seem to be important to follow the recipe for lament psalms. First, acknowledge what God has done. Secondly, state the current stressor(s). Finally, you must reaffirm your faith in God. This is a highly effective form of healing prayer that has a place in the life of every seminary student. It really does work!

God, you called me away
From my old life
To seminary
You have paid all of my bills
And given me time to study
And to begin a new life
With new friends

But these final exams
Have me really stressed out, God
And I don't think that I can make it

With your continual support though, God
I have made it this far
And I know that I will make it
Through these times of trial as well
And onward to a whole new semester.

Christopher C. Randolph
University of Dubuque Theological Seminary
Dubuque, Iowa

A LAMENT PSALM OF CHRISTOPHER RANDOLPH MID-NOVEMBER

God, you told me
To go to seminary.
"Don't worry," you said,
"About how you
Will pay for it, or
Whether you
Are intelligent enough.
You'll like school this time,"
You said.
"You'll do fine.
You won't
Have to go to a big city.
Trust me,
I am your God
And I am with you."

And mostly, God,
My trust
Has not been in vain.
I am in Dubuque,
Not Chicago, Austin, or
San Francisco.
My studies are going well,
I think.
And I do enjoy school now
For the first time
Since I was five.

But though
My long term-finances,
The big bills, are being made,
And I'm (mostly) keeping up
With my class work,
Right now:
I'vegotfourpapersdue;atest
onTuesday;asermonto
preachonThursday;anSPMto
arrangefornextsemester;
I'moutofcoffeeandsmokes;
Ineedtobuyabrandnew,never
usedvideotapeformysermon
onThursday;Idon't
haveenoughgasinmycartoget
homefortheholidays;and
I'veonlygot35centsinmy
checkingaccount.

"Don't worry,"
You tell me.
"I've gotten you this far, and
I'll get you through
This week too.
You've asked me
To help you,
And so I shall.
I am your God
And I am with you.
All your needs will be met."

Christopher C. Randolph
University of Dubuque Theological Seminary
Dubuque, Iowa

DANCING WITH STORMS

Happy are those. . . [whose] delight is in the law of the LORD . . .
They are like trees planted by streams of water.
from PSALM 1

My mood matched the dreary gray skies and the stormy winds blowing outside my window. I watched the large tree twisting in the wind across the way. The leaves turned inside out and upside down, dripping rain like tears. The branches moved violently, changing the entire appearance of the tree, then springing back into shape until another blast of wind bent and changed the tree again.

But the sturdy trunk swayed only the slightest little bit. It moved gracefully, almost as if the wind were its partner in some giant, cosmic dance. The structure of the tree was not threatened by the storm; indeed, it used the rain as nourishment as it funneled the sheets of water down to its roots. Even as its leaves and branches seemed fragile and vulnerable, the tree itself remained strong and steadily used the challenge of the storm to make it stronger.

I want to be like that. I want to dance with the storms of my life as gracefully as my tree. I want to use the flooding torrents to water me and make me stronger. Sometimes the challenges of learning and stretching and growing turn me inside out, twisting everything about me until it seems as if I am upside down. But the whole of my life can still remain sturdy if my roots are deep and my trunk is strong. And if God's Spirit is within me and around me.

Mighty God, your Holy Spirit, wind and water, blows and flows wherever it will. Fill my life with the power of your Spirit so that I, like my tree, can dance with the storms of my life. Amen.

Charlotte Vaughan Coyle
Brite Divinity School
Fort Worth, Texas

FOLLOWING THE WAY OF THE CROSS

Whoever does not take up the cross and follow me is not worthy of me. MATTHEW 10:38

Training to be a minister of the gospel is training to be a theologian of the cross. No Christian theologian has given a clearer description of following the way of the cross than the Protestant reformer Martin Luther. In his "Sermon on Cross and Suffering, Preached at Coburg" (1530), Luther proclaims, "We must note in the first place that Christ by his suffering not only saved us from the devil, death, and sin, but also that his suffering is an example, which we are to follow in our suffering."

Have you ever suffered? Many have suffered the loss of a loved one, failure in the workplace, chronic physical pain, or persecution for religious beliefs. Although suffering is, by definition, never enjoyable, through these pains we are conformed to the image of Jesus Christ, the parable of God to the world. The suffering we experience must not be something we have chosen for ourselves but something we would gladly surrender if possible. God uses suffering to perfect his servants—even his own Son. In Hebrews we read about Jesus: "Although he was a son, he learned obedience through what he suffered" (Hebrews 5:8). Following the way of the cross, we too must hold fast and submit ourselves to suffering, understanding that we must suffer in order to be conformed to Christ. Then, as a parable of Christ, we can minister to others who suffer, sharing the hope of a new life and resurrected body.

Dear God, we commend to thy goodness all those who are in any way afflicted or distressed, in mind, body, or estate: [names]. That it may please thee to comfort and relieve them, giving them patience under their sufferings, and conforming them to the image of Jesus Christ, in whose name we pray. Amen.

Peter Heltzel
Gordon-Conwell Theological Seminary
South Hamilton, Massachusetts

.

REFLECTIONS

When pride comes, then comes disgrace; but wisdom is with the humble. PROVERBS 11:2

As a single parent, I found that deciding to heed God's call to seminary was a financial nightmare. Keeping track of every penny was as much a part of my life as academia! At the end of one semester, in the midst of the stress of finals, I inadvertently paid a $4.00 invoice with a check for the entire balance of my checkbook! Every check I had written bounced like a rubber ball, and the over-payment could not be returned for over two weeks.

The next week, my classmates and I were sharing "end-of-semester" woes. Clearly, I took the prize. I was joking on the outside, but on the inside I was in an abyss of panic. I have always prided myself on my ability to care for myself, and now I didn't even have money to pay for gas!

I rode to my next class with a classmate I knew only through short conversations. As I reached for the car door to exit, she shoved a $50 bill in my purse. I immediately began to protest that this wasn't necessary, that I was really going to be fine. She took my hand and replied softly, "Please do not deny me this gift. Let me do this for you." The look on her face reflected my misplaced pride. I took her gift. It was one of many such gifts of love received during my seminary career. The greatest gift, however, was the mirror that my friend held up for me that day.

O God, thank you for those whom you place in my life that reflect your grace. Help me as I continue to learn to receive from others. Amen.

Terrye Williams
Phillips Theological Seminary
Tulsa, Oklahoma

TRUSTING IS ESSENTIAL

Where can I go from your spirit? Or where can I flee from your presence? If I ascend to heaven, you are there, if I make my bed in Sheol, you are there.   PSALM 139:7–8

When I decided to pursue a calling into ministry and seminary education and discussed it with my spouse, we were scared! After all, this was a tremendous commitment on my part for sure, but it was going to be equally as trying for her and our two children. After several weeks of contemplation and praying for guidance, we agreed that if this was God's call, then we must endure, regardless of how scared we might be.

So, I went kicking and screaming; and thinking that this decision was somewhat irrational because I would be traveling 400 miles round trip from Norfolk, Nebraska to New Brighton, Minnesota every week attending classes. I remember the night before leaving for seminary as being the longest night of my life. There were fears of leaving family, questions about seminary, and anxiety about finances...as well as the recollections of a trusting God whose hand has held me in other uncertain times.

I can hardly believe that there have been four years of traveling, studying, and growing. It has gone fast. To anyone contemplating a call to the ministry, trust your God to be a guiding presence and a God who is with you in the depths of Sheol or at the gates of heaven. Trust in that guiding presence—an everlasting presence.

God, help me to trust in your presence. Help me to remember that regardless of where I go, you are there with me. You are both eternal and ever present. For that, I give you thanks. Amen.

Jeff J. Long
United Theological Seminary of the Twin Cities
New Brighton, Minnesota

GOD, WHO SUPPLIES NEEDS

They brought the jars to her and she kept pouring.
2 KINGS 4:5, NIV

I am a Nigerian seminarian studying for an M. Div. degree at ABSW Berkeley. I began my faith journey with uncertainty on August 13, 1996. I came to the seminary with fears and anxiety. But I had confidence that God would supply my needs. The journey took ten hours. I arrived at Berkeley at night with no idea of where to go. But God sent Saralyn, a senior student, to me. Saralyn saw my anxiety when she gave the key to the commuter house to me for the night. God, who supplies needs, met me at the point of need.

The woman we read about in 2 Kings had a problem. She was unable to pay the debts of her late husband. There was nowhere to turn, and her sons were to be taken into slavery. She saw Elisha, a man of God, and she turned to him for help. Elisha said, "Go round and ask neighbors for empty jars." She obeyed, and there was enough oil to pay her creditors. All her fears and anxiety were gone. God, who supplies needs, met her at the point of need.

Seminarians, old and new, are faced with different kinds of problems, fears, anxieties, isolation, and uncertainty about where to go after graduation. But Jesus has given us the assurance, "I am with you always" (Matthew 28:20). Have confidence and trust in God's promises. Renew your relationship with God through prayers. Students forget to pray due to the pressure to meet deadlines. Have time to talk to God in prayer. The woman trusted God, and she waited patiently until her needs were met. As you pray, patiently wait on the Lord. God will remove the fears and anxieties in your life. God will "renew your strength and mount you up with wings like eagles, so that you will run and not be weary; walk and not faint." Wait on your God, who supplies needs.

Mac Jesuorobo Jatto
American Baptist Seminary of the West
Berkeley, California

GOD DOESN'T WASTE A LIFE!!

If I have won your favor, O king, and if it pleases the king, let my life be given me—that is my petition—and the lives of my people—that is my request. ESTHER 7:3

In a Persian version of our "Miss America Contest," most of the young women in the capital city of Susa were brought to the palace to undergo a year's training to become queen. Esther participated in this training and didn't tell anyone she was Jewish.

At the end of the year's training, all of the young women were presented to the king. Esther was chosen to be the queen of Persia, a Jewish queen in a Gentile country.

Several years later, throughout all the Persian Empire, a decree was issued to kill all Jewish people on the 14th day of the month of Adar, February in today's calendar.

Esther understood her mission when she heard of this decree. At great personal risk, she went to the king, her husband, and begged for her life as well as the lives of her people.

The king agreed, and then was furious with the perpetrator of this decree, which he had signed unwittingly. Esther and her cousin Mordecai wrote another decree that allowed the Jewish population to protect themselves on the 14th day of Adar, which they did successfully. The Jewish Holiday Purim is celeb ted each year honoring Esther for saving all the Jewish people.

Esther stayed her course and saved the Jews. I am sure that she often wondered what she was doing in that harem, until the day came when it became clear to her what she was to do.

Often during the course at seminary, I pose the questions "What does God want of me?!" "Why am I here?!"

Oh Lord, help us stay the course until your plan for us is unfolded.

Susan Scherer
Methodist Theological School in Ohio
Delaware, Ohio

TRUSTING IN GOD'S PROMISE

Those who trust in the LORD are like Mount Zion, which cannot be moved, but abides forever.   PSALM 125:1

On the first day of Middler comprehensive exams, I awoke aware of the anxiety looming just below the surface. The scripture reading for my morning quiet time was Psalm 125, but I never made it past the first verse. It was exactly what I needed to contemplate as I went through the day. The simile is incredibly powerful: if we trust in God—if we put our faith in God and God's promise—we will endure, whatever obstacles and trials come our way.

Of course this does not rule out hardship and calamity. It is during such times that the temptation is greatest to succumb to fear, or resort to our own efforts. However, trusting in the Lord precludes fear—it is simply not a possibility—and yields peace. It also checks our impulses to reach out to other sources of security, all of which pale in the light of God's sovereignty. Moreover, challenges that try our faith in ourselves, and sometimes even God, make for the greatest potential for growth in the Lord (James 1: 3–4). Knowledge of this is especially comforting. It points to our preservation not only temporarily, but eternally.

Lord, be our strength and safe haven, for we put our trust in you.

Charles Echols
Trinity Episcopal School for Ministry
Ambridge, Pennsylvania

THE DIVINE DETOUR

The human mind plans the way, but the LORD directs the steps. PROVERBS 16:9

All of us have dreams and aspirations of what we want to do in life. As I entered seminary, I had dreams of one day becoming a great pastor and leading a local church. The summer following my first year of school I served as an intern in a parish ministry. As I began to get some experience, I started to notice that things were different than what I had expected.

Throughout all of this, I began to ask myself some serious questions that raised some doubts about my future ministry plans. I had experienced the reality of what the writer of this proverb is saying. I had made the plans, but God was divinely detouring me in another direction.

I found myself stubbornly resisting this fact, insisting that God was wrong and I was right. Only as I became broken before God would I experience the true peace and joy that comes with following my Creator.

Are you willing to be "detoured" if God wants you to be, giving up your dreams for God's? You might have your own plans, but only the Lord will know what's best for both you and God.

Lord forgive me when I stubbornly think that I am right and you're not. Help me to accept the fact that as I grow in you, you may have different plans than I do. Give me the grace and willingness to accept your divine detours.

Stephen N. Rath
Asbury Theological Seminary
Wilmore, Kentucky

45

PRAISE TO THE GOD WHO MAKES ALL THINGS NEW

I am about to do a new thing; now it springs forth, do you not perceive it? ISAIAH 43:19a

I began seminary in the month of January. At first it was difficult adjusting to a new city, to new friends and to a new country, not to mention a return to academics after years of working. In the midst of the upheaval of transition, I held on to the promise of God's call. I felt clearly that God had placed me here for a purpose.

Then spring came. As the gentle whisper of the coming spring brushed against my face, my spirits rose. Springtime, with its promise of rebirth and of new life, is my favorite season. I went home for a week over spring break. It was good to be in familiar surroundings and to reconnect with family and friends. When I returned to seminary after my time away, however, I was delighted to discover that it felt good to be back. The campus, the people, and the classes now felt familiar and comfortable. I had made the leap from home to seminary and was finally feeling settled.

Paul tells us in Romans 6:4 that through our baptism we walk in newness of life. God is continually bringing forth new possibilities. In order to grasp the new, we have to be willing to let go of the old. The adjustment period is difficult, but our faith gives us hope that God will use this change to bring forth new life, new fruits, new possibilities in our lives.

God, fill me with the breath of spring, the promise of new life. Open my eyes that I may perceive the new thing you would bring forth in my life, in Jesus' name. Amen.

Nancy Frey
Associated Mennonite Biblical Seminary
Elkhart, Indiana

46

FOCUS

"He has told you, 0 mortal, what is good; and what does the LORD require of you but to do justice, and to love kindness, and to walk humbly with your God?" MICAH 6:8

God has a case against us, accusing us of being unfaithful to our covenant with our Creator. We try to present evidence of our faithfulness: going to Church, giving money, coming to seminary, entering full-time ministry, and so on. But the judge throws out the evidence because these things alone were not part of the covenant. What we have left is our sin and disobedience. God has been faithful, but our sins condemn us as guilty, and the sentence is death. But God intercedes on our behalf and gives God's own Son to die in our place, taking the penalty for our sin so that we can enjoy a close walk with our Lord.

This is a demonstration of God's covenant love. In response we need to make our relationship with God a way of life and not just a ritual. Jesus said to the "religious people" of his day in Matthew 23:23, "Woe to you, scribes and Pharisees, hypocrites! For you tithe mint, dill, and cummin, and have neglected the weightier matters of the law: justice and mercy and faith. It is these you ought to have practiced without neglecting the others." The disciplines of our faith are to be a product of our relationship with God.

Let us remember that the purpose of our seminary education is to mold us into the image of Christ intellectually and spiritually. It is a tool of discipleship that prepares us to serve, as we strive to resemble God's exemplary Servant.

Lord, please teach me to love you with all my heart, mind, soul and strength, and in so doing, to love my neighbor as myself. Shape me in your hands as a potter shapes his clay.

Daniel M. Gurtner
Gordon-Conwell Theological Seminary
South Hamilton, Massachusetts

A MOMENT OF SILENCE

Be still, and know that I am God! PSALM 46:10

Prayer gives me the strength to engage in a journey of faith in answer to God's call. When I pray, I find an awareness of God's loving care for me and for all people; I see the holiness of creation and the face of Christ in every person. Why, then, do I sometimes have to be reminded of the need to pray? Seminary life is often a frenetic attempt to find a balance between the worlds of academia, church, work, and personal relationships. It is easy to get caught up in a whirl of activity. When I am drawn back into prayer, I become centered again—as if I am in the calm of the eye of a storm.

Jesus spoke to his disciples about their need to pray always and not to lose heart (Luke 18:1). My own parish rector tells me to pray often to God for guidance in my vocation. It becomes possible for me to follow this injunction when I see all of my thoughts, words, and actions as a form of prayerful devotion. In daily worship, I join community at prayer. In nature, I contemplate the beauty of creation. In music and dancing, my prayer becomes creative enjoyment and an offering to God. In silent meditation, I am able to find the peace of Christ.

Be with me, God, now and always. With each breath, let me know the wonder of life. Teach me to be still, that I may open my heart to your loving presence.

Audrey R. Woods
Church Divinity School of the Pacific
Berkeley, California

NIGHT

By day the LORD commands his steadfast love, and at night his song is with me, a prayer to the God of my life. PSALM 42:8

The sixteenth century Spanish mystic St. John of the Cross wrote about "the dark where all goes right."

I have chosen a quiet, dark place to kneel down and say prayers, as if I am closer to God surrounded in a womb of darkness. What can I hide in the dark that God does not see? Nothing. But I am purer in the dark. And only my essence and the vast silence lay before me.

"The dark where all goes right," where all secrets are hid from mortal human. No pretense, no excuses; there is only me and God. There is the knowledge that God exists and is present.

In the dark I wait. I am and I am not, so I wait. It is God's will, not mine. I endure the silence, the loneliness, the humility of being human. What I endure is nothing. God is only a memory, held together by faith. I am nothing. I have nothing. I will be nothing. God is everything. My mind yearns for God, searching the dark silence. Then the warmth, the sense of well-being and peace, the union of all and nothing. The light that cannot be put out is given and received. The dark night is painful ecstasy, infinite bliss.

Thank you Lord for the gift of the light that cannot be put out and the knowledge that we always walk as children of that light. Amen.

Drake Whitelaw
Virginia Theological Seminary
Alexandria, Virginia

PRAYING? IN SEMINARY?!!

You would have asked him, and he would have given you living water. JOHN 4:10

When I joined the seminary community, I was so concerned with the eternal destiny of people that I did not bother to ask whether my prayers for them were inclusive. What a shock to be blind-sided by issues such as universal salvation and inclusive language! It felt as if my faith was being diluted, especially during the first year.

Contrary to my expectations, praying actually got more difficult when I entered seminary. I could no longer talk to God as freely as I had before. I worried that I was using the wrong words or that my theology was inconsistent. Worst of all, I worried that I would ask something that might cause others to be oppressed. In a place where God-talk is so prevalent, I often cried, "God, where are you?"

God is "in the search." That has been my discovery over the past three years. It is not easy to find the Holy. However, the deeper we search, the deeper God goes with us. There are moments when we drink of the "living water" in seminary that would never be possible if we did not dig deep and search. So, do not be afraid to dig. God is not.

Present One, do not ever leave me! Go deep into the well with me as I search for living water. Amen.

Charla Gwartney
Iliff School of Theology
Denver, Colorado

PROVOKING ONE ANOTHER

And let us consider how to provoke one another to love and good deeds, not neglecting to meet together, as is the habit of some, but encouraging one another, and all the more as you see the Day approaching. HEBREWS 10:24–25

When I first heard of Covenant Discipleship Groups, I groaned within. I thought to myself, "I don't need one more meeting to attend." I especially resisted the idea that each of us was to be accountable to the group, not only for attending the weekly meetings, but for what we did as Christian disciples between weekly meetings! I thought to myself, why do I need to make a covenant and then tell these people, whom I barely know, how well or how poorly I'm doing in keeping the covenant? Why do I care what they think, and what business is it of theirs, anyway?"

Because these groups were a requirement, however, there was no room for negotiation. The members of the group met and drafted an agreement of things we wanted to do in the areas of devotion, corporate worship, compassion, and justice, to grow in Christian discipleship. One of the activities that we all agreed on was to pray daily for the group members. I will never forget my realization that I didn't want to go to that group and tell them that I hadn't prayed for each of them each day. I was astonished to discover that I did care what they thought and that knowing I would have to own up to my deeds or misdeeds made me very aware of my discipleship (or my lack thereof). Discipleship is not a private individual thing. Provoking and encouraging one another can make a huge difference in our spiritual growth.

God, help us to honestly keep track of where we are in our relationship with you. May we support one another in love and integrity as we seek to do your will.

Priscilla B. Durkin
Wesley Theological Seminary
Washington, D.C.

GROW AS YOU GO!

But grow in the grace and knowledge of our Lord and Savior Jesus Christ. 2 PETER 3:18a

Feeling rushed in your Bible reading and prayer life? As a second year seminary student, I'm learning that I can grow as I go.

Nothing is a substitute for spending consistent quiet time in communion with God and God's Word. "Growing on the go" is additional support. The Bible encourages using every opportunity to learn and meditate on God's Word. "Keep these words that I am commanding you today in your heart. Recite them to your children and talk about them when you are at home and when you are away, when you lie down and when you rise. Bind them as a sign on your hand, fix them as an emblem on your forehead, and write them on the doorposts of your house and on your gates." (Deuteronomy 6:6–9)

I am a full-time seminary student who is married, with four daughters. I spend a lot of time in the car. I purchased the Navpress Topical Memory System to help us all "grow on the go." The scriptures are on cards that you place in a packet which has a view window. I hang the packet from the sun visor in my car. The girls and I have plenty of time to discuss the verse of the day. When they aren't with me, I use stoplights to focus and meditate on the Word. I also use stoplights to lift people up in prayer.

I think the Deuteronomy passage is talking about growing while you're going. It mentions "while you're walking down the road"; I think driving down the road works too!

Lord, help me to use my time to continue to grow in you.

Mary Anne Scheer
Northern Baptist Theological Seminary
Lombard, Illinois

LABYRINTH

You show me the path of life. In your presence there is fullness of joy; in your right hand are pleasures forevermore. PSALM 16:11

Last summer the seminary mowed a labyrinth into the meadow on the property. On a bright day in September the Spiritual Disciplines class dedicated it with scripture, song, and prayer. Then, one by one, we entered the labyrinth and walked the path in silence.

I quickly removed my shoes and began to follow the twists and turns. The soles of my feet felt the ups and downs, the dry twigs, and even something that pierced the flesh. I walked through grass, dry and brown; I walked through grass that was thick, lush, and cool to the touch of my feet. I passed clumps of wild flowers: purple, white, and pale yellow and one incredibly beautiful lavender, star-shaped flower hanging on the end of a tall stalk. The many shades of green were impossible to count. The silence was complete; I was alone in a crowd. In the near distance I could hear the twitter of birds and the singing of insects. In the far distance I could hear the sounds of traffic.

This labyrinth is intended to be a "path to God," a place of contemplation and prayer. These moments were filled with the presence of God. I experienced the "pleasure forevermore," and I felt that "fullness of joy"; and as I walked, tears ran down my face.

O God, you are the source of all good. I thank you for the simple things in life that are full of your presence and consequently full of joy. Let me always walk in the path that leads to life. Amen.

Anita Janzen
Associated Mennonite Biblical Seminary
Elkhart, Indiana

IN PRAYER AND SPIRITUAL LIFE
GOD GIVES THE GROWTH

So neither the one who plants nor the one who waters is anything, but only God who gives the growth.   1 Corinthians 3:7

At the midpoint in my seminary experience, I am less anxious about the "Why am I here?" questions and more resolved to think of the things that will inform my ministry. There are exams and papers, sermons and pastoral care experiences, along with the participatory worship. There is the issue of time management. Specifically, I am aware of the need to be closely connected to God and to nurture that connection.

I address prayer and spirituality, not because I have the answer, but because it is the essence of who we are becoming as future ministers. We must all claim our center in God. In order to do that, we must place ourselves in the private life of prayer and meditation, of scripture reading and quiet contemplation. It may be in combination with walking or running, at daybreak or sunset, in absolute seclusion or in a public setting, but it is essential to allow God the opportunity to give the growth. We all have to be creative people in our intentions to let that happen.

We are all training as servants, working together and finding our way in the place God has for us. As I turn the corner into the final year of my seminary experience, I am less concerned with what lies ahead and more aware of my personal need to be with God. As I draw closer to God, I feel more assured of the source of my nourishment.

Holy God, my growth comes in you alone. May I seek you creatively and daily. In seeking you, O God, I always find what I am looking for. Time with you is holy. Thank you for personal insights that come in quiet moments. Amen.

Debbie Little
Vancouver School of Theology
Vancouver, British Columbia

CLAY POTS

But we have this treasure in clay jars, so that it may be clear that this extraordinary power belongs to God and does not come from us. 2 CORINTHIANS 4:7

In this next-to-the-last academic semester, I seemed to be avoiding something, running away. I was reluctant to own my gifts for ministry. Fearfully, I registered for the one required preaching course. Following my first sermon, the professor confronted me over a lack of trust that God's spirit was present and active in the development and use of my gifts for ministry.

Dismayed, I realized I had been pushing God's gifts, presence, and power away. I had fallen into thinking I was journeying on my own, with only limited help from God. Even after success, I was plagued with a sense of failure. I found myself caught in the lie of human perfectionism and separation from God.

God's "treasure in clay jars" came to mind. I realized the strength and beauty I was working so hard to create on my own were already present, available through God. I could quit struggling, trust, and receive, or I could continue to feel fearful. I am not always successful in remembering that I am a clay pot with God shining through, but when I do, I have an increased sense of possibility and celebration.

Gracious One, thank you for the gift of yourself that shines through us. Help us to remember that your invitation to service includes your loving presence and power, which make it possible for clay pots to be beautifully holified. Amen.

Elizabeth Northen
Perkins School of Theology
Dallas, Texas

ENCOUNTERING GOD

My soul thirsts for God, for the living God. When shall I come and behold the face of God?   PSALM 42:2

Something of the Mystery Is Known

In the beauty of feathered friends:
 the crimson red of the woodpecker looking for food
 the purple sheen of the grackle's feathers
 the courting dance of the sparrows
 and the lively springtime song of the wren.
In the vivid potential of Spring:
 the stately purple iris growing in the bed
 the promise of a pink display of crabapple trees
 and in the unopened flower of the azaleas
 all ready to sing their praises to God.
In the blemishes and scars of life:
 the blind fish in the pond who need special
 care when being fed
 in the difficulty to balance on the limb
 in re-growth following freezing temperatures
 and putting medicine on the wounds of Scruffy
 who knows no home.
In the pink, rose, and gray of the morning sky
 when the eyelid of creation opens with praise
 bringing new time, new love, a refreshing breeze
 which sweeps away old hurts, wounds, and evil
 as the sun rises, thy name is praised.
In the gray sky as the evening's eyelid closes
 drawing the day's activity to an end
 wrapping the sense of time in a shroud
 cinching up the robe on evening chill
 as the evening shutters close, thy name is praised.

Catherine Bennett
Phillips Theological Seminary
Tulsa, Oklahoma

GOD'S PRESENCE

And remember, I am with you always, to the end of the age. MATTHEW 28:20b

My call to ministry all seemed so clear. It all seemed so easy: Go to seminary, graduate, be ordained, and serve a church. To add to our excitement about seminary, my spouse's new job, and a new home, we were also expecting our first child. I was determined that a baby was not going to slow down my seminary work.

But little did I plan on having a baby who would require eight surgeries before she was fifteen months old. Danielle needed so much attention and love. I was ready to quit seminary, but my husband convinced me to lighten my class load. However, for weeks I just went through the motions and struggled to feel God's presence.

After I completed my first semester, Danielle was four months old and had to have open heart surgery. The night before her surgery, I was unable to get to sleep. Then as I thought about Danielle's surgery, I began to sob. My husband awoke and placed his hand on mine. I then experienced what felt like a huge embrace enfolding both of us. God was present, and I experienced that presence in a very revelatory way. God's embrace did not assure me that "everything was going to be okay" but, more importantly, that God was always with me—something I had forgotten.

As I continued on with seminary (and two more children), I was constantly strengthened by this experience and the assurance that God is always with me. When God seems absent, it is not God's absence but rather my inability or unwillingness to notice God's presence.

Loving God, help me to always feel your presence. No matter how busy, overwhelmed, or tired I might become, help me always to stop in your glory. Thank you for being present. Amen.

Elizabeth Hadler
United Theological Seminary of the Twin Cities
New Brighton, Minnesota

AS THE WINTER'S CHILL

O send out your light and your truth; let them lead me; let them bring me to your holy hill and to your dwelling.   PSALM 43:3

As the winter's chill
Draws its clammy blanket
Around the dead and falling leaves
Of my faith
That worked so well
In my comfortable summer home
I doubt and wonder.
Why did you call me here?
To lose my faith on this Holy Hill?
I am so exposed here.
Glib words won't do.
People look me in the eyes here
And ask what is in my heart.
Is this what you meant?
For me to exhaust myself?
To spend the last ounce of my strength?
To become so empty
That I must find sustenance in you?
So weary
That I must find rest in you?
So needy
That I need only you?
O Lord, I am empty.
Fill me with your love.
I am weary.
Hold me in your unchanging and everpresent arms.
I am needy.
Teach me to find all I need in you.

Marty Conner
Virginia Theological Seminary
Alexandria, Virginia

GOD, ARE YOU STILL THERE?

My God, my God, why have you forsaken me? Why are you so far from helping me, from the words of my groaning? PSALM 22:1

I am in the midst of my third and final year of seminary. When I answered God's call into ministry, I had no idea what I would be in for. My wife and I moved three hours from our home and family, expecting a highly spiritual and satisfying life on campus. It was a rather rude awakening to find that everything I thought I had learned about God and the Bible was about to be fed through a threshing machine. We were thrust from a comfortable church home to an environment that left us feeling empty and alone.

It did not take long for the feelings of desperation to set in. In fact, I felt as though God had abandoned us...as though God had said, "Listen to me: You're going into ministry. Move away, go to seminary, and look me up when you get out." How could God have done this to us? God led us here...how dare God leave us high and dry in the meantime? In all of my prayers to God, I felt that I was being ignored.

It has taken some time, but I have come to realize more fully that God is indeed with us all the time. God suffers when we suffer, and rejoices when we rejoice. It is when we feel most isolated from God that we are in fact being held tightly within the arms of God.

Gracious and eternal God, please help me to have patience. Help me to understand what I am going through and how close you are by my side, even during the times I feel distant. You have brought me here O God, and I know you could never forsake me. Amen.

Douglas A. Griger
Saint Paul School of Theology
Kansas City, Missouri

59

AND THE WORD SPOKE

All scripture is inspired by God and is useful for teaching, for reproof, for correction, and for training in righteousness, so that everyone who belongs to God may be proficient, equipped for every good work.   2 TIMOTHY 3:16–17

There are certain moments that fall neatly into the realm of human experience; and then there are moments that defy the normal patterns of human experience. When I responded to my call to ministry and started my seminary experience, I soon realized that this moment was inspired by God's will. The living reality of God's will came to me in moments of sharing in the spiritual community; pursuing academic goals with other seminarians; building caring, compassionate relationships with the Dean and faculty leadership; contemplative prayer; and long hours of theological reflection and biblical study. In the midst of these spiritual encounters, I reached the understanding that God is present in all moments of life and is blessing all of us in the same time.

From these experiences I reached a spiritual awareness that God spoke to me always; sometimes God spoke through other seminarians, professors, or related spiritual encounters. In the crucible of seminary life I experienced moments when "the Word became flesh," and God spoke to me about the message of promise and hope in Jesus Christ, our Lord and Savior.

Dear God, awaken my senses to your teaching, guidance, and training, that I might serve your church in obedience to your word alone.

Ulysses S. Payne
Howard University School of Divinity
Washington, D.C.

60

YOUR FIRST SERMON

But before all this occurs, they will arrest you and persecute you....
This will give you an opportunity to testify. I will give you words
and a wisdom that none of your opponents will be able to with-
stand or contradict.   LUKE 21:12–15

Well, you haven't been arrested and thrown into prison. No! You had to go one better than that. You went to seminary, and now you're in your first preaching class. And all too often, you think that prison would have been the preferable choice! For you're drowning in work from your other courses, and now you have to prepare, and deliver, a sermon. It looks so easy when your pastor preaches. She speaks effortlessly, and every word out of her mouth seems to drip with meaning. But it's your turn now; it's starting to look as if preaching isn't as easy as she makes it seem.

You've interpreted the passage for weeks! You've written, and rewritten, and spent what seems to be hundreds of hours preaching the final rewrite to an empty sanctuary. And now it feels as if you're not prepared at all. For you're standing in the pulpit in front of a sanctuary that's no longer empty. Your mouth feels like a desert. Your knees are almost visibly shaking....

The service is over now, and a line of people are waiting to shake your hand. Most of them smile and say, "Nice sermon. I enjoyed it so much!" But others stop to really speak to you. You realize that despite your fear, you had spoken the word, that God's spirit plucked from your lips and twisted to God's purpose. Wisdom that your ability did not create. Wisdom that could not be withstood or contradicted.

Forever may the words of my mouth, and the meditations of my heart, be
acceptable in your sight, O Lord, our rock and our blessed redeemer. Amen.

Frank Fisher
McCormick Theological Seminary
Chicago, Illinois

PROCLAIM

Now go, and I will be with your mouth and teach you what you are to speak.   EXODUS 4:12

I am a Vietnamese American seminarian studying for the Diocese of Evansville, Indiana (which consists of mostly Anglo-Saxon Americans). Because I am naturally shy, one of my most terrifying fears is of public speaking, not to mention in a foreign tongue. If anyone would ask me the question, "Why then did you decide to become a priest?" my answer would probably be, "I don't know." It is true that in reality there is no logical answer for my being in the seminary studying for the priesthood. Yet my desire to be a priest is as real and alive as ever. Perhaps one can look at it as a "calling." God has a specific plan for my life, and I am simply following it without questioning or looking for a logical explanation.

In the midst of preparing to be future ministers of the church, one of our most important job descriptions is to be good public speakers. For many of us, public speaking causes fear, but this fear can be overcome. Every time we step up behind that pulpit, we are staring that fear in the eye. Every time I get ready to go to the pulpit, I remember a comforting passage where Moses said to the Lord: "But I am slow of speech and slow of tongue" (Exodus 4:10). Then the Lord said to Moses, "Now go, and I will be with your mouth and teach you what you are to speak."

Lord, be with my tongue and teach my mouth to speak of your goodness. Let me realize that it is you, not I, who speaks to your people through my mouth and my tongue. Amen.

Joseph Hoang
Saint Meinrad School of Theology
Saint Meinrad, Indiana

PROCLAIMING THE WORD OF GOD

Then I said, "Ah, Lord GOD! Truly I do not know how to
speak"....But the LORD said to me, "...you shall go to all to
whom I send you, and you shall speak whatever I command you,
Do not be afraid of them, for I am with you to deliver you," says
the LORD. JEREMIAH 1:6–8

Giving that first sermon is a challenge
To feel confident in proclaiming God's word
To feel able to communicate it.

Don't we all feel like Jeremiah?
How can I do it? How will God's word be proclaimed?

I felt it.
The questions, the doubt, the overwhelming inadequacy.

Yet, throughout the experience
God's reply to Jeremiah is God's reply to us.
I am there, says God.
Proclaim what I say to you; speak the Word!

We are not alone.
The Holy Spirit will speak to us
And guide the words we offer to God's holy people.

We are called
Both priest and laity
To proclaim God's word to the world.

God of grace and glory, fill us with your spirit
So that our tongues may proclaim your word!

Kurt J. Huber
Church Divinity School of the Pacific
Berkeley, California

WHO AM I TO SPEAK FOR GOD?

Such is the confidence that we have through Christ toward God. Not that we are competent of ourselves to claim anything as coming from us; our competence is from God, who has made us competent to be ministers of a new covenant, not of letter but of spirit; for the letter kills, but the Spirit gives life. 2 CORINTHIANS 3:4–6

I have answered God's call, left the life I knew, and come to seminary to study and prepare for ministry. My heart is full of love for God and my hands prepared to serve. God has given me gifts of public presence, a strong speaking voice, skills for writing and wonderful stories to share. But when asked to write a sermon and prepare to preach, I am filled with doubts and fear. All of the papers I have written here at seminary have been about religion and theology, but this assignment is different. I am not being asked to talk *about* God. Who am I to speak *for* God?

The task seems overwhelming, but the assignment is not the problem. The "I" is in the way. My sinful human ego is the stumbling block. The only freedom that will make the assignment possible is my acceptance of reality: The task is not mine. As the text says, I am not competent, but I can be confident that God will give me what is needed for the task. I cannot claim to speak for God, but God will give me the words to speak. God gives the gifts. God will make me competent to speak, and the Spirit will give life. I need not fear. The words are not mine, but God's.

Lord, I am broken and sinful, but I am here to serve you through ministry. Be with me as I write and prepare to preach this sermon. Calm my fears and let me know with confidence: My competence will come from God, and the Spirit will give life. Amen.

Melinda Melhus
Luther Seminary
St. Paul, Minnesota

THE PRICE OF LEARNING

It is good for me that I was humbled, so that I might learn your statutes.   PSALM 119:71

It seems as though the pursuit of the seminary degree is as much an academic endeavor as a spiritual journey for those preparing for ministry. Something happens between the responsibility of visiting a parishioner in "post-op" and studying the effects of "post-modernity." Something causes the warm and pathetic student minister to become a G.P.A. economist. The assignments, the exposure to new areas of thinking, competition, and interaction with diverse groups of people are all part of the seminary experience. From time to time I have been distressed by the challenge to perform academically while also searching out an appreciation for ministry and its practical demands. Academics can simply press the wind out of one's vision of ministry. However, the irony in this sometimes frustrating struggle toward academic training is that God seems to have intention, purpose, and plan.

Perhaps what an anonymous poet said is true: "The farmer plows through fields of green and the blade of the plow is sharp and keen; but the seed must be sown to bring forth grain; for nothing is born without suffering and pain; and God never plows in the soul of humanity without intention and purpose and plan; so whenever you feel the plow's sharp blade, let not your heart be sorely afraid; for like the farmer, God chooses a field from which is expected an excellent yield; so rejoice though your heart be troubled and broken in two. God seeks to bring forth a rich harvest in you."

God, help me to trust that you are bringing forth a rich harvest in me. Please turn my burdens into the nourishment which will make that harvest bountiful and ease my tired soul. Amen.

Walter Spears
Memphis Theological Seminary
Memphis, Tennessee

CHILDREN OF THE LIGHT

For once you were darkness, but now in the Lord you are light. Live as children of light—for the fruit of the light is found in all that is good and right and true. EPHESIANS 5:8–9

I was taking my first seminary class focused on the New Testament. The first half of the quarter was focused on the epistles, and I had been trying to understand the relationship between the law and the saving work of Christ. I was to turn in a paper on this topic, but I felt I was getting nowhere.

I was encouraged in another class to spend an hour in prayer, walking the campus grounds and finding a place for contemplation. It had been a while since I had prayed for this long, but after some difficulty I became very centered, reflective, and open. But my thoughts kept returning to the relationship between the law and Christ. As I was walking back to class, I passed family housing and saw my son playing in the yard. His face lit up as he saw me, and we hugged one another.

In a flash, my confusion cleared away! In my son I saw an eagerness to love that did not result from obligation. A loving disposition is superior to any law, no matter how good. While I had heard this many times before, I hadn't really understood it on a deeper and more personal level. My academic difficulty was overcome when I explored it in an attitude of prayerful reflection, being open to God's grace.

Source of Wisdom, help me to remember that although logic and reason are required in my studies, it is prayerful reflection that leads to receiving your wisdom.

Steven Putka
Methodist Theological School in Ohio
Delaware, Ohio

FOCUSED—ON WHAT?

I bless the LORD who gives me counsel; in the night also my heart instructs me. I keep the LORD always before me; because GOD is at my right hand, I shall not be moved.   PSALMS 16:7–8

After more than a thirty years' absence from university study, I am in seminary. My return was overwhelming; would my brain still function in "serious" areas after spending years reading *Parenting Magazine* and *Cat in the Hat*? Undergraduate study was competitive even then, but if you studied hard and worked like a maniac, you could make the all-important grades. When I returned to school last year, I wet my feet by taking one class each semester. With both sons in college, I had the time to pursue my "grade goal," even with a full-time job. But this year, with full-time classes....

I came home after the first day completely overwhelmed by the syllabus in each class—the reading, the "recommended" reading, the papers, and the exams! How can I do all of this and still do it "well"? I felt as if I was weeks behind after my first day! But our older son cut to the point: "Mom, remember why you are there." Do we sometimes forget that we are not here to garner the grades, the honors, the recognition? Do we need the occasional gentle (and sometimes not so gentle) reminder that we are here doing God's work and learning how to do it better? Do I need to remember that sometimes keeping the Lord always before me is done in Community Chapel and Seminary Singers, not the library?

I love the learning, the study, and the friendships, but not the performance pressure of exams! And when it's overwhelming, I need to remember why I am here—to answer God's call, not mine.

Holy One, keep your presence before me to keep me focused on your purpose for my life.

Virginia Falconer
Perkins School of Theology
Dallas, Texas

REACHING FOR THE ROCK

In distress you called, and I rescued you; I answered you in the secret place of thunder; I tested you at the waters of Meribah.
PSALM 81:7

Part of my sense of call is deeply connected to study. Of scripture, surely, but also of the history of the church and of its shifting role in culture. Yet, that study is often driven by anger at a word that keeps escaping my efforts at translation, at some alternative ecclesiology that I find just plain obnoxious, at the occasional texts written in the jargon of therapy and self-actualization so appealing to the twentieth-century church professionals, at a slippery idea that I can't seem to figure out how to express in words.

And yet, and yet...God is so much *here* in this work, in these ideas, in these words and texts. Striving to be revealed to us, coaxing our fuzzy brains, along with our reluctant hearts, to search for truth, encouraging our imaginations with the ongoing story of God's work in our history, ultimately conquering our anger and our frustration. In these words, between the boards of our books, we again encounter the mysteries of God. There is glory here; there is wonder here. Here we can find the "honey from the rock" that nourishes and enchants.

My life flows on in endless song; above earth's lamentation,
I hear the sweet, though far-off hymn that hails a new creation.
Through all the tumult and the strife, I hear the music ringing;
It finds an echo in my soul — How can I keep from singing?
The peace of Christ makes fresh my heart,
A fountain ever springing;
All things are mine since I am Christ's!
How can I keep from singing?
From *Bright Jewels for the Sunday School,* Robert Lowery, 1869

Melissa Kirkpatrick
Wesley Theological Seminary
Washington, D.C.

BIBLE STUDY

Of making many books there is no end, and much study is a weariness of the flesh. ECCLESIASTES 12:12

Mark Twain once said something to the effect that it was not those things that he did not understand in the Bible that bothered him but rather the things that he did understand. My belief in the fallen state of humanity is such that I would be surprised if nothing in the Bible bothered me, if indeed it is the word of God and I am human. Nevertheless, it was what I could not completely comprehend in the Bible that led me to seminary. Studying is something I am comfortable doing, and it was convenient that it coincided with my faith.

Historical curiosity and the demands of a seminary curriculum foster the desire to "study to shew thyself approved" (2 Timothy 2:15, KJV). At times, however, God gets lost in the details of exegesis. A healthy fear of taking anything out of context sometimes results in a paralysis that prevents God's word from being heard here and now. It thus takes less-than-active hostility to some of scripture's contents to stifle its transformative potential. It is easy to put off an honest encounter with the Word under the conscientious pretense of consulting one more commentary. But the two need not be contrary. While much in the Bible remains obscure and requires our diligent study, as Twain reminds us, more than a little of it is clear enough to convince us that we do not ultimately judge God's word, but rather that "it is able to judge the thoughts and intentions of the heart" (Hebrews 4:12c).

Lord, grant me a mind capable of familiarity with your word without the contempt it sometimes breeds. Teach me humility and hope with all that I learn. Amen.

Patrick Gray
Candler School of Theology
Atlanta, Georgia

KNOWLEDGE IN PERSPECTIVE

Knowledge puffs up, but love builds up. Anyone who claims to know something does not yet have the necessary knowledge; but anyone who loves God is known by God. 1 CORINTHIANS 8:1b–3

I once knew someone who referred to seminary as the "cemetery," and I can sometimes relate to why one would offer this cynical comparison. I went to seminary because of a deep sense of calling and a profound awareness of the presence of God in my life. Once I began, though, two circumstances often caused me to stumble. One was getting caught up in the materialism of the quest for high grades and to be knowledgeable as an end unto itself, which the artificial system of rewards and punishments at seminary tended to encourage. The second was having my belief system challenged and sometimes contradicted by the facts and theories presented in the classroom.

Now, as I approach graduation, I believe that God has helped me to put my education in perspective, and I offer this advice: Do not let the study of theology replace the practices which energize you spiritually. It benefits us not to trade knowing God for speculative knowledge about God. Also, the ways of God are mysterious and not fully knowable by our limited human minds. Do not let the overturning of some of your fixed or preconceived ideas shatter your faith, but rather allow yourself to be open to new understandings. When you encounter new uncertainties, be confident in your experiential knowledge of God, the God whose presence you have felt and who has called you to seminary.

Loving God, help me to not lose sight of you in the midst of completing endless assignments. Help me to know your presence, even in my uncertainties and fears.

Pratik K. Ray
Harvard Divinity School
Cambridge, Massachusetts

PRESENCE

O God, you are my God, I seek you, my soul thirsts for you; my flesh faints for you, as in a dry and weary land where there is no water. PSALM 63:1

It is the last week of the semester before exams. I got up early this morning to go worship God in the seminary chapel, beginning a nineteen-hour day in which I spent most of my time reading about God, thinking about God, even daring to write about God. But in the whole course of that long day, not once have I felt God's touch, not once have I heard God speaking to me. How could I? I have four models of atonement to memorize. I have to look at Deuteronomy 6 to see what principles of Hebrew syntax are operating in this (normally) stirring passage. I have to examine rhetorical devices in someone else's sermon.

Most of this is necessary work. In my ministry I will need to have ways of speaking about Christ's sacrifice on the cross for us. I will need to be able to unlock meanings in the Hebrew scriptures that might not come through in my NRSV translation. And I need to be able to use language artfully to bring my sermons to life. Right now, though, I want God, not words about God.

I try to pray, but I don't have any words. It seems as if all the words I know have been painstakingly extracted from me and fed into my computer, processed into papers. My best, most glowing words have found expression in my sermons. So now I am speechless before the One I most want to speak to. But God knows that there are sighs too deep for words. In these wordless sighs, I suddenly find release, comfort, healing: peace. I know that God is there even when all I can do is turn my attention to God with inarticulate longing. I don't have to utter a word, or wait for a word. The thirst of my soul, though never quenched, is watered.

Lisa Kenkeremath
Virginia Theological Seminary
Alexandria, Virginia

71

IMPERATIVE WONDER

After three days they found him in the temple, sitting among the teachers, listening to them and asking them questions. LUKE 2:46

Wonder. See it as a noun if you wish, a state of mind attributed to children. Sit in wonder in a darkened cineplex. Buy a season ticket to a theme park, line up, and wonder if this ride, this enormous mouse in gloves, will remind you of that wonder you were told you could reclaim here.

Or treat wonder as a verb, imperative. A commandment: wonder, you.

How? Ignore little, attend much, and ask. Unmask the trappings of knowledge: the merit scholarship, the final letter grade. Employ, but don't revere these. Cultivate your ignorance until it blooms as curiosity. Begin with "I don't know." Begin with "what if," the way God did: What if I breathe across the deep, or breathe into the soil, or pull a bone from a man and make a woman?

Begin with "I don't know." What if you look ignorant?

So what if you look ignorant? You are, but less so, maybe, than that junior-high-aged Jesus, who wondered with the rabbis in the temple in Jerusalem. *All who heard him were amazed at his understanding,* which was conceived in unknowing and made flesh in questions. Jesus' curiosity was godly. It was God's.

And yours? Is it concealed beneath a basket woven of embarrassment? Have you silenced your questions in fear that your uncertainty is faithlessness and sin? Take courage. Think of Jesus questioning his teachers, and ask what you don't know. Pray to the God who wanders in the garden, who wonders aloud, "Where are *you?*" Ask. Your questions are wonderful. They're one way of saying, in faith, "Here I am."

Rachel Srubas
McCormick Theological Seminary
Chicago, Illinois

TAKE TIME TO MAKE TIME!

Listen! I am standing at the door, knocking; if you hear my voice and open the door, I will come in to you and eat with you, and you with me. REVELATION 3:20

Making time in my schedule to spend with God has been a struggle for me. As a ministerial student one would think that this would come naturally; however, with all of the reading and paper writing it is oftentimes difficult to allow oneself time to nourish one's own soul. I have often felt guilty for taking time out just for me, but I have learned that unless I take the time, I will not be as healthy spiritually as I need to be in order to serve others as I wish to serve. As the saying goes, "You can't help others until you learn to help yourself." I feel this is especially true in a field that calls us to serve and help others. If we do not first learn to nourish ourselves, how will we then be healthy enough to care for others?

One of the ways I have been able to make time in my schedule is by having a spiritual friend. We meet weekly and discuss our reading material and what's going on in our lives, and we pray for one another. Having a partner to travel with has been an enriching experience. Not only do I have someone who holds me accountable for my spiritual nourishment, but we have also developed a close friendship.

As a student I know the demands of school, church, and a part-time job, and finding time without guilt and impatience is not easy. However, I have seen the difference both in myself and in my work as I have allowed time for God in my life outside of the assigned readings of school.

Gracious God, be with me as I struggle to spend time alone with you. I know how much I need you; help me to find the way.

Lesleigh Carmichael
Vanderbilt Divinity School
Nashville, Tennessee

PEACE AMIDST CHAOS

I have said this to you, so that in me you may have peace. In the world you face persecution. But take courage; I have conquered the world! JOHN 16:33

Berkeley is a crazy place to live! There is absolutely no shortage of diversity, social causes, and outrageous personal expression. In a city that is just a stone's throw away from San Francisco, where I am convinced that almost anything is possible, it is easy to be consumed by the overt physical, visual, experiential, and spiritual stimuli that beg for attention and demand from a seminarian's already limited amount of time. There is so much I want to do, so much I want to stuff into three short years. Who knows if I'll get the same opportunities when I leave seminary and the Bay Area, and, heaven help me, pastor a church! At times I am convinced that I have to do everything now. I live in a state of urgency.

But my soul calls me to be still. To wait. To treasure silence in a bustling city that buzzes throughout the night and in a bustling schedule that barely allows sleep. I am called to make and keep priorities. The most important of these priorities is my relationships with God and the people around me. Seminary can make people feel scattered and diffused. Through silence and prayerful meditation, I feel more connected to God—the reason I am in seminary. And by connecting myself deeply with God, my relationships with others reflect peace and sincere earnestness.

Guiding and Graceful God, be my peace. Help me to be a calming presence, a peacemaker, in this restless world. May my actions manifest patience, integrity, and the incalculable value of human relationships. Amen.

Christy M. Newton
Pacific School of Religion
Berkeley, California

ENDURANCE

Not that I have already obtained this or have already reached the goal; but I press on to make it my own, because Christ Jesus has made me his own. Beloved, I do not consider that I have made it my own; but this one thing I do: forgetting what lies behind and straining forward to what lies ahead, I press on toward the goal for the prize of the heavenly call of God in Christ Jesus. PHILIPPIANS 3:12–14

Several years ago my home church started a new tradition for Epiphany Sunday. During worship, baskets are passed by the ushers, and within the baskets are paper stars, each with a different written word. The idea is to make that word yours for the year, finding how it relates to your life and your faith.

This year, my word was *endurance,* a particularly apt word for this time in my life as I participate in the frenetic juggling act that is the life of so many second-career seminary students. I was reminded of that word tonight as, exhausted from a day at work and anticipating a night of study, I sank onto a seat on the bus.

The good news is, we *can* do all things through Jesus Christ who strengthens us! I have found that even at my most tired or discouraged, the grace of God will suddenly be revealed to me through kind and encouraging words, an inspirational sermon, or even simply a hug from a loved one. And I remind myself of those last words of Jesus to his disciples as recorded in Matthew: "And remember, I am with you always, to the end of the age" (Matthew 28:20). Endurance can be ours, if we hold fast to that promise.

God, give me the strength to go on, to press forward to my goal of serving you in ministry. Help me to remember always that you are the God of steadfast love, and that you are always with me.

Mary E. Morrison
McCormick Theological Seminary
Chicago, Illinois

PRIORITY

Be still, and know that I am God! PSALM 46:10a

"How many times have I heard that verse?" I wondered, as I looked at my wall calendar. On that calendar I saw an image of a man on a seacoast, sitting comfortably on a pillar of rock, with a sky full of angry clouds behind him and those words etched into that dark and brooding sky.

"I couldn't sit comfortably there," I thought, seeing how dark that sky is and knowing how long it would take me to climb down from that pillar.

Having just endured one of the most frenetic weeks of my four years in seminary, pastoring a church, trying to stay connected, or at least recognizable to my family, and seeking to fulfill the requirements of my academic schedule, I felt that the sky in that background looked an awful lot like my state of mind right then. How could he just sit there?

Then the words came clear. They were printed in subdued hues, not boldly splashed across the page. They were artfully done, so that your eye constantly wanted to come back to them, away from the central image of the man on the pillar. They called to my eyes, and the more I looked at the image, the less I saw of the pillar and its occupant.

"Yes Lord, I hear You."

Lord Jesus, still my racing heart and mind, calm me as I walk with you, because of your love for me. Remind me that you are exalted above the earth, above schedules, above demands and needs; my only need is you, Lord Jesus. Thank You!

Thomas D. Snyder
Ashland Theological Seminary
Ashland, Ohio

FLOWING WATERS

There is a river whose streams make glad the city of God, the holy habitation of the Most High.   PSALM 46:4

I sit staring at the piles of unread books, incomplete papers, scribbled notes, and blank applications lying on the floor of my bedroom, and I wonder how I will ever get everything finished. Waves of frustration sweep over me. The day does not hold enough time for completing all that is before me. I have materials to prepare for the seminary's fall retreat and letters which need to be mailed inviting students to participate in our community activities. Did I remember to call my ministry committee for my senior interview? My calendar says I have not. I need to write an article about a retiring professor for an upcoming seminary publication. How will I find time to write the last of my exegesis for class? When did I schedule my Old Testament presentation? Oh, no, I've discovered that I have no clean socks.

My head is spinning. My stomach is in knots. I am overwhelmed not only with the huge amounts of work I have, but decisions about my future weigh heavy on my heart as well. Oh, where is God now? Even with the window blinds closed, I know it is dark outside because I am once again awake at 3:00 a.m. I begin misting the palette tray with moisture, and I watch the watercolors soften. As the paints glisten with water, I am struck by how once hard, dry surfaces have become ready for use. I dip the bristles of my artist's brush into the softened blocks of color. The brush strokes cause the indigo blues to flow into the sea greens. The picture of a babbling mountain stream becomes visible as paints move across my canvas. The waters of painting are a reminder that God's spirit flows within me. The spirit softens my heart. God is present. My busy schedule has kept me from being still. Taking the time to create a painting has brought me closer to God's peace.

Marilyn Nash
McCormick Theological Seminary
Chicago, Illinois

GARDENING

You shall be like a watered garden. ISAIAH 58:11b
They shall make gardens and eat their fruit. AMOS 9:14d

Gardening in the spring provides such renewal for me—getting my hands into the rich, loamy soil and working it until it is ready to accept the new plants, or the seeds for this year's blooms.

When I'm in my garden, I am always reminded of the cycles of life. There is always a beginning, a middle, and an ending. Sometimes the middle can be called chaos, yet out of that chaos always comes a new beginning.

Sometimes the cycles start with an ending and move through the middle time, or through the chaos and then into the beginnings: the beginnings of a new career, the beginnings of a new life, children born, grandchildren born, and SUDDENLY it is all clear. The light shines upon us and we know why we are in seminary— we know why God wants us here.

Gardens have been with us since the beginning of time—Adam and Eve lived in the Garden of Eden. Gardens have always been part of the biblical lives and times that we know about.

The cycles of life refresh us and help us to know our Lord and to understand that there is always something for us, in the next cycle, or in the one after that.

Seminary life has so many demands on us, all of our time, resources, strength, and often our soul. Gardens refresh us. And seminary life ends up providing us with the fruits of its own garden, the garden of learning, that we must plow through in order to serve our Lord.

Oh Lord, help us to till your soil so that we may be refreshed and learn of your good works. Amen.

Susan Scherer
Methodist Theological School in Ohio
Delaware, Ohio

HOLY GROUND

Then God said, "...Remove the sandals from your feet, for the place on which you are standing is holy ground."   Exodus 3: 5

As a student intern at a Connecticut prison, I have a pass that permits me to go about the prison compound unaccompanied. Every time I enter the facility, my bag is searched. I step through a metal detector, and an electronically operated door slides open. I enter a small area where employees pick up and drop off keys at the beginning and end of each shift. Another door slides open, and I step into a reception area where the correctional officer on duty unlocks a door that allows me to enter a waiting area. Through two more doors, I arrive at the prison compound.

My time here is spent in personal contact with prisoners, listening to them and praying with them. I am privileged to hear the secrets of their hearts, without sitting in judgment. Our small group Bible studies are blessed times of sharing. There is no need to be afraid. The prisoners look forward to my visits, a contact with someone who brings them God's love.

I have discovered that the prison compound where I walk is holy ground. The suffering is great. God's presence is palpable. I see Christ in the faces of the prisoners I meet, and this nourishes me spiritually. A sacredness surrounds my visits with these prisoners as I listen to their stories and pray with them.

Tender God, you see the affliction of your people and hear their cries. Grant me a willing heart, always ready to respond to your call to minister to the least of these who are members of your family. Amen.

Charlotte White
Yale Divinity School
New Haven, Connecticut

GOOD NEWS PROCLAIMED AMONG US

There is a boy here who has five barley loaves and two fish. But what are they among so many people? JOHN 6:9

This past summer I met LuAnn while working as an outreach minister for the Ecumenical Night Ministry in Chicago's inner-city. LuAnn is 35 and dying of AIDS. Yet, though her end is near, she never ceases to smile, her face radiating serenity and tranquillity. Her younger sister, Barbara, however, seems to struggle with her sister's coming death. An illiterate mother of four, she depends on LuAnn for much more than sisterly love. While LuAnn spoke with me, Barbara stood behind her, clutching and embracing her, and sobbing on her shoulder.

LuAnn, however, continued to glow, caressing her sister's hands and speaking softly, "Don't worry, things will be all right." In that moment Martin Luther's words, "Just as there is in the midst of life, death, so is there in the midst of death, life," were made real for me. I realized that within LuAnn is a true understanding of the gospel's promise of life eternal. It is an understanding based on the certainty that there is always hope, if one only trusts in God, and that things will always be "all right" if one believes they will be.

LuAnn's neighborhood, with its crumbling houses, panhandlers, and drug dealers, is far different from my comfortable university environment. Too often, like Andrew in this text from John, I may not believe that those who seem to have so little can satisfy the spiritual hunger of many starving believers. But by meeting others where they are and letting them share with us their stories of how God is working among us, we can all be nourished by this good news—the true bread from heaven.

Lord, open us to the ways you are continually witnessed to and proclaimed among us. Use us to spread these stories to others.

Michael E. Karunas
University of Chicago Divinity School
Chicago, Illinois

IN THE PRESENCE OF THE LORD

Then Jacob woke from his sleep and said, "Surely the LORD is in this place—and I did not know it!" GENESIS 28:16

O ne of the greatest joys and greatest frustrations of seminary has been the church that calls me pastor. When I came to seminary, I had already had the privilege of serving a congregation during my undergraduate work. I had learned much from that little congregation in Missouri. Foremost, I had learned how to be truly part of a community that reflected the love of Jesus. I came to seminary with confidence that I had experienced the presence of God in the church that I had served.

Then, I was called to pastor another small church, this time in Kentucky, where I was going to seminary. I found a congregation that was different and with whom I was much more easily frustrated. For the first time in my life, going to church on Sunday was a struggle for me. Then one day, as I spoke to one of my professors, he said to me, "Jill, just continue to pray that God will enlarge your heart that you can love them more."

The realization that began in that moment and that has continued to develop over the last two years is that it is not up to me to decide whether these people are worth ministering to. God has already made that decision. Maybe the situation is different from what I had experienced before, but God is present in that place. The love of God is extended as much to people in that church in Kentucky as it is to me or to anyone else. And now I can say with confidence, "Surely the LORD is in this place."

Gracious and Loving God, it is your presence that refreshes me, your presence with me that washes me in your vast love. Remind me that you are ever present with all of your creation.

Jill Cameron Kaylor
Lexington Theological Seminary
Lexington, Kentucky

THE WALK BETWEEN

They said to each other, "Were not our hearts burning within us while he was talking to us on the road, while he was opening the scriptures to us?" LUKE 24:32

Theological education, for me, has been a continuous struggle between the realm of ideas and the realm of "doing dishes," the sometimes tedious work of ministry. At a recent conference I attended on urban ministry, I found myself walking back and forth between this conference and another one that was more "ideas-centered" taking place a few blocks away. I enjoyed both places. But I felt alone in the walk between. My walk (or bike ride) between seminary and my field placement also highlights the contrasts between ideas and the grittiness of life. Noticing God's presence in both places is challenge enough, but the walk between, where I prepare my mind, heart, and spirit for the transition about to take place, is sometimes even more difficult.

The story of the Emmaus Road helps me reflect on my "walk between." After their commute on that dusty road, the disciples ask in retrospect, "Were not our hearts burning within us?" At first, they did not notice God's presence with them on that road. Part of my own growth is learning to pay attention to my "burning heart" in the unexpected, dusty, and routine places of life. It is at those places that I need to sit up and take notice of the Christ who is walking beside me and then go and follow in the breaking of the bread and in "doing the dishes" of ministry.

God of all creation, teach me to notice you today in the unexpected places. In all those times when I least expect to notice you, may your Spirit cause my own heart to burn within me. Amen.

Ben L. Hartley
Boston University School of Theology
Boston, Massachusetts

PASSING THE PEACE

For the sake of my relatives and friends I will say, "Peace be within you!" PSALM 122:8

H e was a new patient, scarred from recent surgery but bearing wounds that were much older. He wanted to attend Sunday mass but hesitated because, "I know I'm not good to look at." I wondered at that; he was not obviously disfigured. He elaborated: "I've seen ugly things." His story evoked battle scenes that I had heard described before. "Are you a Vietnam veteran?" I asked. Yes, he was. "So am I," I said.

He stared at me for a moment, then invited me to sit down. He told me about the horror that had left him confined to a wheelchair, followed by the desolation of returning home to find himself regarded as a pariah. I asked if that was the reason he thought he was ugly. He just nodded his head and looked away as he caressed his useless hand.

I observed, aloud, that the gentle spirit shining in his eyes had not been destroyed by that ugly time. Quiet for a moment, he suddenly looked at me, raised his left arm and saluted. I recalled my aversion to that military symbol and my joy at leaving it behind so many years ago. Then I looked into his remarkable eyes, felt his great longing for acceptance, and standing at attention, returned the best salute I could muster.

Healing Spirit, help me to be a source of peace for those who have lived too long in turmoil. Amen.

Patricia Yorke Robinson
Andover Newton Theological School
Newton Centre, Massachusetts

VISITING THE SICK

He heals the brokenhearted, and binds up their wounds.
PSALM 147:3

The summer after my second year of divinity school, I did an internship in Clinical Pastoral Education (C.P.E.) at the Veteran's hospital in Nashville, Tennessee. I heard rumors of the dreaded experience of C.P.E. and showed up my first day not knowing what to expect. Would this experience knock my foundation of faith out from beneath me? Would my soul be ripped from my body? I am happy to say that neither of these two things happened to me; and I came away from the summer with a deeper understanding of my own faith and a heightened sense of spirituality and ministerial purpose.

As a chaplain, I worked with pre- and post-surgical patients and their families. Through wonderful, thought provoking supervision sessions with peers and my encounters with patients, I came to realize that one simple, fundamental kernel of knowledge persisted in every visit. My supervisor stated it so succinctly: that caring, affirmation, and appreciation are the greatest gifts we have to share with those to whom we minister.

God grant that I can be caring, affirming, and appreciative of all your gifts and creations.

Jason Gottman
Vanderbilt Divinity School
Nashville, Tennessee

FIELD MINISTRY

But when the disciples saw him walking on the sea, they were terrified, saying, "It is a ghost!" And they cried out in fear. But immediately Jesus spoke to them and said, "Take heart, it is I; do not be afraid." MATTHEW 14:26–27

I chose to endure the adventure known as Clinical Pastoral Education. I worked for a summer in an acute care hospital as a chaplain-intern. Simultaneously, it was a frightening, grace-filled, and rewarding process. One of the most significant learnings for me was that "ministry of presence" is not just being there for a patient. It is a *real* ministry because the pastoral visitor who gently enters the patient's and/or family's space brings the compassion that is witnessed in holy presence. And God is a very present reality.

As I have experienced it, the ministry of presence required in any form of pastoral work is at least threefold. There is being present to ourselves. C.P.E. is a depth encounter. By coming face-to-face with myself—*my* fears, *my* reactions, *my* talents, and *my* theology—I was more able to offer the hospitality of an unencumbered presence to others. There is also being present to God, to be available to be used to communicate God's love and concern.

Jesus demonstrates being present to others as he says, "Take heart, it is I; do not be afraid." The disciples, as their boat was tossed about in chaos, were so wrapped up in their own fear that they temporarily missed the grace extended to them in Christ. But he was there, and he was concerned. Through self-encounter and holy-encounter we are energized to encounter God's people.

Help me daily, O God, to be present to myself, to you, and to others in a spirit of Christian hospitality. Direct my paths by your Holy Spirit and lead me through my fears to love. Amen.

Thomas A. Flint
Drew University Theological School
Madison, New Jersey

THE PLACE OF PERSPECTIVE

But when I thought how to understand this, it seemed to me a wearisome task until I went into the sanctuary of God; then I perceived their end. PSALM 73:16–17

It has been in seminary that God has expanded my understanding of what it means to worship God, of the many ways our expressions of worship delight God's heart. Entering the sanctuary of God to present offerings of worship is one of the most precious experiences we can have; and indeed, every moment we may enter the sanctuaries of our hearts and worship God. We were made to worship God, and in worship we fulfill part of our very purpose.

Sometimes, in the midst of trials or crises, or in the midst of the casual living that threatens to take over when we become preoccupied with the endless stream of urgent matters before us, we lose sight of the importance of this time of worship. But it is in this time of worship that we are given the perspective to deal with everything else in our lives. We give our praise to God; and we are reminded that the Lord is our God, worthy of praise, and that God has a plan and a purpose for our lives. It is in worship that we remember and celebrate the One who gives us that life.

Lord Jesus, I need your perspective in order to live to the fullest this life you have given me. As I worship you, please show me how you view my life, my time in seminary, my relationships, and my future. Help me not to neglect that essential time in your presence.

Katharine A. Brown
Gordon-Conwell Theological Seminary
South Hamilton, Massachusetts

BEFORE YOU GIVE UP

Jesus said to him, "No one who puts a hand to the plow and looks back is fit for the kingdom of God."   LUKE 9:62

I can recall two times during my seminary career when I wanted to quit, to just drop out. Oh, it was hard! So many things were clamoring for and taking my attention away from the holy work God was calling me to do: to be in school and learn. Each time, it was the above verse that shook me enough with its truth that I pressed on toward graduation.

Jesus' words to the would-be disciple were sharp. They are words that I have needed to hear as well. The most anxious times of seminary, for me, were when I attached a "but" to my Christian vocation. How often have I looked back to the haunts of past experiences, human limitations, and the details of circumstances (e.g., student loan debts) in order to avoid future responsibility.

I have found that a personal vision is needed to survive the rigors of theological education and ministry. There needs to be a point to it all. Just as on a compass, a point—something on which our gaze is fixed, a goal—allows us a direction to follow. My "point" has been the *possibility* of becoming the Christian leader I believe God intends for me to be.

The farmer plowing the field keeps his or her attention focused on the holy ground directly ahead, not on either side, and certainly not on that which is in the background. Be the one who diligently engages in study and practice. Be the one who keeps your hand on the plow no matter what. Be the one who trusts in God.

Most holy God, show me the true point toward which I am struggling. Help me to avoid the detours I notice along the way. Bless me with direction so that I may follow Jesus' steps. Amen.

Thomas A. Flint
Drew University Theological School
Madison, New Jersey

SECURE IN GOD

You are always with me, and all that is mine is yours. Luke 15:31

God, come to my assistance! What am I doing here? My class-mates appear to be so intelligent, so articulate, so spiritual, and so confident. My course work seems beyond comprehension. Have I gotten in over my head? Should I even be here?" These doubts and insecurities often plague me.

I try to tell myself that, of course, there will always be someone who is more such-and-such than I. However, my own voice offers only temporary satisfaction. But then I hear God's comforting voice: "You are always with me, and all that is mine is yours." God says to me, "My child, where does your heart look? When it looks to others first, then it is natural to be insecure. I am calling you to be secure in me. When your heart looks first to me, you can be confident in the knowledge that I am always with you and that all I have is yours. I love you, have given you all that you need, and have called you to share your unique gifts with others." When I can truly believe this voice of God, I will know true security.

I have discovered in conversations with friends that these doubts are not unusual. It is difficult to admit that one is insecure in an environment where great value is placed upon security and self-confidence. However, it may be more difficult to confess one's inse-curities to God. Yet this is what we are called to do, for only by emptying ourselves of pride can we be truly secure in God.

God, thank you for loving me and calling me to serve you. When I feel unsure of myself, help me to turn to you, so that I may be secure in you alone. Amen.

Andrea Wong
Yale Divinity School
New Haven, Connecticut

SILENT PRAYER

My help comes from the LORD, who made heaven and earth.
PSALM 121:2

I entered seminary late in life. It started with a difficult three-day trip from Spokane, Washington, to the community of Midway in southern Tennessee. Finally, one dark night in August, I drove the Budget rental truck, dragging my worn Volkswagen Jetta, up the driveway toward a little reddish-brown house in which the electricity and water had been turned off. I was fifty-two years old. Classes were to begin three days later. The reading lists and assignments were dauntingly impossible, and I did not own or know how to operate a computer. I felt lost. Moreover, I began to question my abilities and my decision to leave the insurance business and enter seminary. Had I made a terrible mistake? Had I hopelessly misunderstood what I thought was God's will for me?

Anguish and self-questioning persisted. Yet prayer took on a new importance. During a course in pastoral practice, the chaplain of the University of the South introduced me to a different kind of prayer, centering prayer. When praying this form of prayer, I would read a psalm and then listen in silence, saying nothing for extended periods of time. I would dismiss with a "sacred word" any thought or emotion that entered my consciousness. The idea was to listen and hear what God was saying. I began to sense deeply within me that God looks over us and calms our anguish. To hear and feel God within us, we must first quiet ourselves and listen.

The Lord shall watch over your going out and your coming in, from this time forth forevermore. Amen.

Paul Phillips
School of Theology, University of the South
Sewanee, Tennessee

FOOLS FOR CHRIST

Fools say in their hearts, "There is no God."   PSALM 14:1a

One of the tasks of seminary education is to develop in the future minister a fuller knowledge of God. From the outside, that makes perfect sense. But for a first-year seminarian, the process of having every beloved story, cherished belief, or "unshakable" foundation of faith blasted away is terrifying. You begin to question even the most basic beliefs. You wonder, "What am I doing here? What kind of pastor will I make if I can't say for certain there is a God?" And you feel very much the fool.

These times of doubt are not to be avoided. Allow yourself to examine each belief; see what you have mistaken as the foundation of your faith. You will discover that even though God is not in whirlwinds, earthquakes, or fire (nor in brilliantly executed exegesis, an A in Hebrew Bible or completeness of Systematic Theology), God is still there with you—a still, small voice that until now had been muffled beneath all those other bits of stuff you thought were faith.

Don't try to go through this alone. Keep a journal. Talk about what you're experiencing with someone you trust. Practice being open and vulnerable. Trust God-With-Us to be involved even when you don't sense God there at all. And remember how it felt; someday, someone else will need to hear how you came through it.

God be with us, because sometimes seminarians are such foolish people. Amen.

Nancy L. Moore
Boston University School of Theology
Boston, Massachusetts

U.B.U.

They came and filled both boats, so that they began to sink. But when Simon Peter saw it, he fell down at Jesus' knees, saying, "Go away from me, Lord, for I am a sinful man." Then Jesus said to Simon, "Do not be afraid; from now on you will be catching people." When they had brought their boats to shore, they left everything and followed him. LUKE 5:8–11

As seminary students, we tend to say, "I wish that I could preach like him," or "I wish that I could offer pastoral care like her!" God called *you* to be *you,* in service to the Lord, with the gifts and graces that were given to *you*! If the Creator wanted two of the other person, then two of them would be in seminary instead of you. Accept the gifts that God has given you, so God can give you more! God called you "just as you are," and if changes are necessary, God will accomplish that as you grow. The key is simply, "U.B.U."

We are God's chosen ones. You have been called from among the sheep to be a shepherd. By the sheer act of submitting yourself to give up the life you had before seminary, you have taken the first step to truly being yourself through Christ. Some will accept the change that God offers gracefully, and others will be broken and beaten down by the transforming experience of seminary. When we are willing to do it Jesus' way, it turns out better than we could have expected!

Dear Lord, I will follow you. Help me to set aside my agenda and listen closely to the plans that you have for me. Thank you for accepting me "just as I am." Now, Jesus, change me into what you would have me to be to serve you better. Amen.

Ed Brady
University of Dubuque Theological Seminary
Dubuque, Iowa

GOD LOVES YOU AS YOU ARE

And a voice came from heaven, "You are my Son, the Beloved; with you I am well pleased." MARK 1:11

Going to seminary for me required taking a major leap of faith. As a Christian man who also happens to be gay, I had struggled for years to understand who I was in light of the gospel of God's unconditional love. Did my soul's worth rise and fall solely on the few isolate passages of scripture that some wield as a (self-) righteous sword, or did God make me—me!—with something greater in mind? In answering the call to ministry, I elected to step out on faith that God indeed meant to take me as I am into God's service—that not despite, but because of, my truth, I could serve Christ's church in its seeking and finding God's Truth.

What truth(s) do you bring along with you into ministry? Do you dare divulge it all and put all that you are into Christ's service? Jesus, our fully human, fully divine Savior, began his ministry by being baptized by John in the muddy waters of the Jordan along with throngs of regular folk — imperfect types like you and like me. Jesus learned his true identity at that moment, that he was the beloved of God. As baptized Christians, we too have been consecrated to God's care and service; in that moment God claimed us as faithful daughters and sons, beloved for all time.

All of who you are is precious to God; in baptism God loves us as we are. Trust your truth. Be yourself. For in being authentic you will best serve God and God's people.

Jesus, give me the courage to use my truth in faith, that in so doing I might witness to your Truth, which is love.

Read Scudder Sherman
Harvard Divinity School
Cambridge, Massachusetts

BIG AND SMALL

Are not two sparrows sold for a penny? Yet not one of them will fall to the ground apart from your God. MATTHEW 10:29

During winter break, I attended a Christian cruise featuring inspiring seminars with legendary pastor and radio preacher Dr. Jack Hayford. As a seminarian and a new pastor of a struggling congregation, I was excited to discuss "church talk" with Jack.

"I've got to get my sermon ready for Sunday," Pastor Jack mused. "I'll probably have ten to twelve in worship." "Hundreds?" I asked remembering his impressive congregation. "No," he answered. "Thousands! What about *your* flock?"

"I'll probably have ten to twelve in worship, too," I replied. "Hundreds?" asked Jack with his eyebrows arched in surprise. "No," I said with some remorse. "Just ten to twelve."

Together we chuckled, and Pastor Jack began to tell me of his earliest days of ministry. Although his congregation is large today, it wasn't always that way. Pastor Jack began pastoring over twenty-five years ago with just a hundred persons. During that time, God multiplied his congregation to 10,000–12,000 in worship weekly.

In a big, big world, it's easy to feel dwarfed by all of the surrounding largeness. Yet God's word speaks often of the importance of even the smallest things: a tiny mustard seed, a poor widow's minute offering, and even the smallest of Jesus' fans—children. Big or small, God uses us all!

Lord, teach us to always be mindful that no tiny detail (or congregation) escapes your watchful eye. Amen.

Mona Oei Safley
Louisville Presbyterian Theological Seminary
Louisville, Kentucky

IN THE MOMENT

Do not fear, for I have redeemed you; I have called you by name, you are mine. ISAIAH 43:1b

So much in seminary is future-oriented. How will I meet all the deadlines? What classes shall I take next term? What will my next sermon focus on? How am I going to spend the summer? What about after graduation? Where will I be? What is next?

I find myself constantly living in the future tense, contemplating questions I am not yet ready to answer. How easy it is to forget the present in preparing for the future. But it is the present in which I encounter the living God; I am alive now, not tomorrow. This moment, vibrant and fleeting, offers a window onto the divine presence: It is sufficient. Instead of asking "What is next?" I should ask "What is now?" Until I learn to inhabit the present, I will hardly be able to be present to others in my ministry.

Each moment is an opportunity to plunge through the surface distractions into the presence of God like splitting thin ice. If I trust in the God who is, the worries appear for what they are: grasping for what is beyond my control. Instead, may I let the God who calls me by name lead me to the answers moment by moment.

Eternal God, so often my focus strains to make out the future instead of seeing clearly what is. Great I AM, you invite me simply to be, and thus to be fully alive in every moment. Let my fears dissolve in the immediacy of your presence.

Dwight Zscheile
Yale Divinity School
New Haven, Connecticut

TIME OUT!

The sabbath was made for humankind... Mark 2:27a

As a student intern at Connecticut Hospice I was touched by the many "Sabbath" experiences I shared with patients. I would sit by a patient's side and share in a celebration of the life he or she had lived. For many, it was the first time they had ever stopped long enough to rest and reflect on their past. We spoke of joy and pain, gains and losses, hopes and shattered dreams. Each life story I heard created a sacred space of remembrance and celebration of a life nearing its end. I found that most of my patients led lives that were focused predominately on the future. Now that death was near they often regretted waiting so long to celebrate the past.

Like any person, the life of the seminarian is filled with expectation for the future. The promises are of new classes, field placement, possible ordination, and the future life of ministry. In the midst of all this planning for the future, God is calling us to take a time out! Before we lose track of our lives by continually looking to the future, we are called to take time to rest and reflect on the creation of our lives. Doing this, I began to recognize the many ways in which God worked in my life to provide me with opportunities and guidance. This in turn allowed me to become more comfortable trusting my Creator to provide for my future. So take some time out today. Celebrate the creations and blessings that have taken place within the last week of your life. Remember, God created the Sabbath for you too.

God, help me to take a time out. Help me, through times of Sabbath reflection and rest, to celebrate the life I have been given. Amen.

Brian S. Gerard
Yale Divinity School
New Haven, Connecticut

GIVING UP CONTROL

But he said to them, "It is I; do not be afraid." JOHN 6:20

In many ways, the years at seminary have been some of my most enjoyable. Hearing distinguished faculty lecture, experiencing a relevance between academics and work in a congregation, and sharing struggles with colleagues about the nature of faith are all opportunities that may never again be afforded me. Yet in other ways, seminary has been difficult.

How easy it is to get carried away by a self-centered mentality. We may tend to compete with one another in the classroom, basing our self-worth on the grades we receive. We may focus so strongly on reaching goals that we miss the beauty of time spent with friends. We may search for control of our lives, overwhelmed by those around us who appear to have discovered the answers to life's most difficult questions. Moreover, it is perhaps only after we satisfactorily accomplish what we set out to do that we make room and time for the presence of Jesus Christ.

But what if we do not have the answers or feel we are not in control? What about those preparing for graduation, who feel uncertain of what the future holds? They may struggle, not knowing where they will be, or what they are called to do. This text from John can offer reassurance. Though we, like the disciples, may want Jesus to come into our boats where we are confident and secure, he remains upon the stormy waters. But in offering the words "Do not be afraid," he comforts us. For if we trust enough to venture out from our safe places into those that seem uncertain and vulnerable, there will we find Jesus. For he is waiting for us to discover him there. To be within the control of God is far more certain and secure than anything we can control ourselves.

Michael E. Karunas
University of Chicago, Divinity School
Chicago, Illinois

96

ENJOY EACH DAY!

This is the day that the Lord has made; let us rejoice and be glad in it. PSALM 118:24

It is so easy in seminary life to lose the joy of the day by becoming preoccupied with the future: finishing a book, writing a paper, studying for an exam, moving from one deadline to the next. As a second-year seminarian, I've found that there are a myriad of questions to answer and choices to make regarding the future: classes, internship, placement, and so on....

Being prepared for the future is necessary, but *living* in the future can create anxiety. I have found that when my eyes become too focused on the future, I sometimes miss the unexpected surprises today can bring. Each day brings opportunities for laughter, joy, relaxation, and restoration, but sadly, days slip by when I am too busy, preoccupied with thoughts, plans, and preparations for the future, to notice.

Sometimes when I'm feeling anxious, I find myself thinking things like, "I will feel so much better once this paper is done; I will feel so much better once this exam is over; I would be so happy if all my reading was done; I would be able to relax if I was past preaching my first sermon."

The future is full of unanswered questions and challenges. King Solomon's answer to this would be to recommend allowing joy and contentment each day to encourage us during our journeys. "So I commend enjoyment, for there is nothing better for people under the sun than to eat, and drink, and enjoy themselves, for this will go with them in their toil through the days of life that God gives them under the sun" (Ecclesiastes 8:15).

Lord, help me realize the joy that each day brings!

Mary Anne Scheer
Northern Baptist Theological Seminary
Lombard, Illinois

DARE TO DREAM

And he dreamed that there was a ladder set up on the earth, the top of it reaching to heaven; and the angels of God were ascending and descending on it.   GENESIS 28:12

There is something wonderful and magical that occurs when one's mind is first touched by a dream. Dreams evoke those most sacred and sublime feelings as our mental chords are struck by the beauty of thoughts heretofore unknown. As the rays of the sun warm and illuminate as they touch and tingle the skin, so does the mind as it is enchanted by the encounter with that which is wholly new and different. A sweet potpourri brews and comes to entice the senses as eyes once closed become aware of a new possibility. Such is the nature when the wonder and majesty of the human psyche is impacted by the splendor of the mysterious dream.

Throughout our theological education, we will inevitably find ourselves perplexed and puzzled by the complexities of academic life. As our attention is drawn toward the goals and objectives of our course work, we must become ever more watchfull not to let our mental landscapes become impoverished by the absence of dreams. Dreams enrich our minds and our souls and empower us to continue to strive toward goals we thought were unattainable. The luminous quality of dreams opens a myriad of possibilities and replenishes the spirit with a sense of beauty, a sense of presence, and a sense of hope. Throughout our seminary experience, we must hold on to dreams so that their splendid radiance will embolden us to look upon the world with bright eyes and open hearts.

Eternal Thou, grant me the peace to rest and replenish in the wonder and majesty of dreams.

Corey D. B. Walker
Samuel DeWitt Proctor School of Theology
Richmond, Virginia

THE EXODUS PATTERN AT GRADUATION

The crowds that went ahead of him and that followed were shouting, "Hosanna to the Son of David! Blessed is the one who comes in the name of the Lord! Hosanna in the highest heaven!"
MATTHEW 21:9

Springtime in Jerusalem is no stranger to celebration. Springtime means the Passover. The Passover celebration means calling to remembrance the great actions of God on behalf of God's people. We celebrate God's decisive purchase of a people for God's self, the desert trial proving God's faithfulness, and the joy of God's outstretched promise of an eternal inheritance. This is the exodus pattern: Celebration becomes trial, and trial turns into eternal joy.

Jesus also understands the exodus pattern. He approaches Jerusalem during the springtime celebration. Upon a donkey, he enacts the promise of the prophets. There is celebration, intense joy. "Hosanna!" The Lord saves the people! Jesus does not stop here. He follows the exodus pattern into trial. Trials of public controversy, slander, betrayal, public humiliation, the apparent abandonment of God. Yet, he does not stop here. The exodus pattern turns into eternal joy as the Son in whom God delights receives resurrection and eternal inheritance. This is the exodus pattern: Celebration becomes trial, and trial turns to eternal joy.

Lord, teach me now about the exodus pattern. Strengthen my heart to experience the fullness of celebration. Let me drink of your goodness and remember your faithfulness at this graduation. Stand with me as I enter periods of trial. Let me know your provision in the desert, your protection from public disgrace. Fix my eyes upon the surety of your future promise. Let me thirst for your presence and the inheritance of your eternal joy. Amen.

David L. Palmer
Gordon-Conwell Theological Seminary
South Hamilton, Massachusetts

THE ROAD AHEAD

I will instruct you and teach you the way you should go; I will counsel you with my eye upon you.   PSALM 32:8

Fortunately I enjoy traveling because, like a lot of people, we live many miles from parents, siblings, and friends. I enjoy driving and, even though we have traveled certain networks of highways many times, I like to prepare for a trip by taking a look at the map and making sure I have a good mental picture of where I am about to go. One particular route winds its way through the Allegheny Mountains on a two-lane road before smoothing out and widening into four-lane comfort. This two-hour stretch of road requires focused attention since there are a number of turns that, when missed, will lead a traveler into strange and unfamiliar places.

In a similar way, as I prepare for my final semester of seminary studies, I realize that finding my way into the future ministry God has prepared for me requires a familiarity with the map that is God's Word and an attentiveness to the signs that are representative of God's voice as I hear God speak through the counsel and encouragement of those who know me well, through the circumstances in which God has placed me, and through that still, small whisper I hear from within. I need a vehicle that has been serviced and fueled for the trip. That vehicle is my body, which must be tuned with spiritual disciplines and prayer, fueled with good physical care including exercise and sensible eating habits, and maintained with mental and emotional wellness.

Make me to know your ways, O LORD; teach me your paths. Lead me in your truth, and teach me, for you are the God of my salvation; for you I wait all day long.   Psalm 25:4-5, NIV

Twila K. Yoder
Eastern Mennonite Seminary
Harrisonburg, Virginia

THE END IS NEAR, OR IS IT?

May the God of steadfastness and encouragement grant you to live in harmony with one another, in accordance with Christ Jesus, so that together you may with one voice glorify the God and Father of our Lord Jesus Christ. ROMANS 15:5–6

What a bleak morning: no sun, only bitter cold, and I must order the books for my next class. God, I thought four years ago that the non-traditional route to a seminary education was the best way for me. There were lots of variables, and all seemed to fall in place. I never thought I could see it through, but today, when the new semester enrollment arrived in the mail, your light reflected from the envelope, and as I opened it your grace and consequential joy flowed almost visibly. There are only three classes and a thesis yet to secure. How did this happen so fast? How can it be possible that two of my classmates are ordained and two more are making preparations? Many others have come and gone, but you have given me the strength to stay. Why? I am never going to bring thousands to your kingdom or fill the coffers of a cathedral with the elegance of my words. My promise to you, though, is that I will serve faithfully and, if need be, follow the paths of those of the "old circuits" and keep the remote and marginal in your fold. Until I heard your call, I was just a middle-aged mother, teacher, farm wife, and now I am complete.

God, I know this is not the ending but rather the beginning, and I am so excited I can hardly contain myself. It is most difficult, for there are few to share my joy, no classmate at the exact same point, just friends to reach by phone or letter. Yet, that doesn't matter because you know the joy you have given me and the path you have chosen. When you offer your call you also provide the way, the means for us to answer. For all the many mini-miracles, thank you. I will always feel your presence. Amen.

Phylicia Hart
Eden Theological Seminary
St. Louis, Missouri

CARRYING IT TO COMPLETION

He who began a good work in you will carry it on to completion.
PHILIPPIANS 1:6b, NIV

This is the last semester of school. Looking at all the unknowns that follow graduation, my old career begins to look pretty good. I made a comfortable living at that job; I understood what was expected of me, and I knew my strengths and my limits. This new work is laden with risks. What if the first call turns out to be a misfit? What if I fail my exams? What if I'm not approved for ordination? It's too late to go back; my finances are a mess; after graduation I have nowhere to live. What will I do? How will I eat? "What have you done to us, bringing us out of Egypt?"

And then I remember my internship experience, tasting what it's like to be used of God. I remember that this work, even the work of preparation, is not accomplished by my efforts alone. I remember that this calling includes God's promises, as well as God's demands. "He who began a good work in you will carry it on to completion."

God will be faithful. All this worry, all this fear, only comes when I expect to meet all the challenges myself. Like those Israelites in the desert who tried to save extra manna, I seek security against an uncertain future. I forget my vesselship. After three years of study, learning to depend on God's active involvement in all aspects of my life may be the most valuable lesson of all.

Forgive me, Lord, for the times when I forget your providence, for the times when my little-red-hen instincts overshadow my dependence on you. May I be receptive to your nudges. May my actions reflect your involvement. Amen; alleluia.

Mary DeWolf
Louisville Presbyterian Theological Seminary
Louisville, Kentucky

LEADING WITH YOUR LIFE

Let no one despise your youth, but set the believers an example in speech and conduct, in love, in faith, in purity. 1 TIMOTHY 4:12

Having recently graduated from Ashland Theological Seminary, I am in the uncomfortable position of looking for where God wants me to be next. God has called me to pastoral ministry, that much is clear, but where I will be next is not so clear.

As I have spoken to church leaders, one question has come up that interests me greatly: "Do you think your age will be a problem?" As of this point I am not yet twenty-eight years old, and some of the congregations I would be interviewing with consist of people whose children are older than I am.

The answer to the interviewer's question can be found in 1 Timothy 4:12. Timothy was a young man facing the task of being a spiritual leader in a congregation. Paul instructs Timothy not to worry about his age, perhaps since he can do nothing about it, but to concentrate on the quality of his life. Timothy is to be an example in the way he lives his life for the church he is entrusted with.

I have a note above my desk that reads "We lead with our lives not just with our lips," to remind me that I have to watch not just what I say, but also how I live.

God, thank you for choosing us to lead your church. We humbly accept your call. Help us to be the people we need to be to your honor and glory.

Arthur C. Carr
Ashland Theological Seminary
Ashland, Ohio

LOVE, KNOWLEDGE, AND INSIGHT

And this is my prayer, that your love may overflow more and more with knowledge and full insight to help you to determine what is best. PHILIPPIANS 1:9–10a

When I was in seminary, graduates often came back and said something to the effect of, "They don't teach you *that* in seminary!" Sometimes it was said as a complaint about the seminary curriculum, other times with a note of awe about the unpredictability of ministry. When I was a new pastor, a colleague and I joked about the merits of a class that dealt with issues such as robes, stoles, and how to tuck your shirt collar into a clerical collar!

In this age of information and specialization, it was difficult in seminary for me to choose which area of knowledge and insight was most important. Should I take a second class in preaching or study influential theologians of the early church? Pastoral care for the dying and grieving or further study of Hebrew or Greek? Difficult choices to make while exploring my call!

Since graduation, I have grown in appreciation for the time and freedom seminary provided to read and discuss specific issues and subjects thoroughly. This year I have been surprised to see myself make connections between seminary-gained knowledge and experiences in the church that may at first seem unrelated but worked to blend love and insight. Perhaps that is grace: that God will use our unique interests, experience, and knowledge in surprising ways for the good of the kingdom.

God, help me to use my head, my heart, and my body for your service, combining love and the insight of the rich traditions and bodies of knowledge that guide the care of your people.

David D. Colby
McCormick Theological Seminary
Chicago, Illinois

HOPE

I consider that the sufferings of this present time are not worth comparing with the glory about to be revealed to us.
ROMANS 8:18

I wondered, out loud sometimes, Is there life after seminary? I had spent six long years pursuing my Masters of Divinity. Theory up to the eyelids. Would it ever be of practical use? However, I did not expect what I got in my first four months in the parish ministry. I was called upon to perform twenty funerals, give pastoral care to multiple terminal cancer patients, and respond to the cries of many hurting and lonely persons! It seemed like an endless stream of stories of grief and hopelessness.

Almost before I unpacked my first box of books and even had a chance to decide which shelf they would adorn, I had to ask myself, "How does hope come to the hopeless?" The apostle Paul does not deny this suffering but instead finds hope in it. Hope is in transcending the reality of what is into the possibility of what can be. Hope is in the power that raised Jesus from the grave. Hope is in those who trust in a faithful God.

God, teach me to share the hope found in your presence. Let me model care, nurture, and love. Help me to practice resurrection. Amen.

Brooks Barrick
Christian Theological Seminary
Indianapolis, Indiana

LIFE AFTER SEMINARY?

For surely I know the plans I have for you, says the LORD,...to give you a future with hope. Then when you call upon me and come and pray to me, I will hear you. JEREMIAH 29:11–12

I began my last semester of seminary with mixed emotions. Although I was eager to complete my M.Div. degree, I was anxious about the future. Where would God send me? I was so anxious, in fact, that I was somewhat paralyzed by my fear. As demands were being made for my time and attention there seemed to be less and less "me and God" time. There was so much to do and so little time! I was completely overwhelmed.

For a brief moment in time, I had forgotten—forgotten that God had indeed called me to ministry. I had forgotten God's promise to me that my Creator would never "leave or forsake me."

In those final hours of trial and self-doubt, we are wise to follow Jesus' example. Take a bold step and meet God face-to-face in the garden. Venture out into the wilderness, away from the safety of your seminary walls. Whether it be a weekend retreat, an overnight camping experience, or an afternoon in a park, invest your time in "being with God." Allow your Creator to share in your anxiety, anger, and fear. After all, isn't that what Jesus did?

As you make final preparations for your continuing ministry, as one chapter closes and a new one begins, remember that God has called you for a purpose. Practice patience, and all will be revealed to you in God's time. You were called to be a servant of God. God will continue walking with you beyond those seminary walls.

Gracious God, I trust that you are with me and have granted me gifts to be shared in Christian ministry. Calm my fears O God, that we may continue to walk together. Amen.

Alison Phillips
Christian Theological Seminary
Indianapolis, Indiana

Index